William Howard Russel

Hesperothen

notes from the West

William Howard Russel

Hesperothen
notes from the West

ISBN/EAN: 9783744650823

Printed in Europe, USA, Canada, Australia, Japan

Cover: Foto ©ninafisch / pixelio.de

More available books at **www.hansebooks.com**

HESPEROTHEN;

NOTES FROM THE WEST:

A RECORD OF A

RAMBLE IN THE UNITED STATES AND CANADA
IN THE SPRING AND SUMMER OF 1881.

BY

W. H. RUSSELL, LL.D.

BARRISTER-AT-LAW.

IN TWO VOLUMES.

Vol. II.

LONDON:

SAMPSON LOW, MARSTON, SEARLE, & RIVINGTON,

CROWN BUILDINGS, 188 FLEET STREET.

1882.

LONDON :

PRINTED BY WILLIAM CLOWES AND SONS, LIMITED,

STAMFORD STREET AND CHARING CROSS.

CONTENTS OF VOL. II.

a 2

CHAPTER V.

KANSAS TO ST. LOUIS.

CHAPTER VI.

NEW YORK—NEWPORT—DEPARTURE.

CHAPTER VII.

RETURN TO EUROPE.

CHAPTER VIII.

SOME GENERAL REFLECTIONS.

CHAPTER IX.

THE RED MAN AND HIS DESTINY.

HESPEROTHEN.

CHAPTER I.

ARIZONA.

Deming—The Mirage—Ruined Cities—American Explorers—Self-Tormentors — Animals and Plants — Yuma — California — Los Angeles—Santa Monica—The Pacific.

May 30th.—At an hour as to which controversy might arise, owing to the changes of time to which we have been subjected, the train, which had pulled up but seldom during the night, stopped at Deming Junction, where the Atchison, Topeka, and Santa Fé Railroad "connects" with the Southern Pacific, on which our cars were to be "hauled" to San Francisco. Jefferson time and San Francisco time differ two hours, so at one end of the station we scored 6 A.M., and at the other 8 A.M. The sooner one gets away from Deming in any direction the better. A year ago—as is usually the case hereabouts—there was not a trace of a town on the dry ugly plain covered with prickly acacias and "Spanish bayonets"; now Deming flourishes in gaming and drinking saloons, express offices, and all the horrors of "enterprise" in the West. The look-out revealed a few tents, wooden shanties, a station, at which work-

men were running up a frame-house, ground littered
with preserved provision tins, broken crockery, adobes
and refuse of all sorts. At the door of one hut,
swarming with flies, swung half a carcase of beef; two
women were washing, pale-faced, but not uncheerful
creatures, who had not a good opinion of Deming and
its population. "They carry out a dead man a day, or
used to," said one informant. The lady washerwomen
did not quite corroborate the figure; but, remarked the
chattier of the two, "there was a considerable shewtin'
about last night!" To the observation of one of the
party that he was "going to have a look about," the
other lady made reply, "I guess if you dew it will be
'hands up' for ten cents with you." On the platform
was a United States marshal, with a revolver stuck in
his belt, but his duties were considered to be punitive
rather than preventive. Here Mr. Chase and Mr.
Hawley left us to return to Topeka. At the abschied-
nehmen Sir H. Green was affected by a proof of
interest in his welfare of a touching character and
very full of local colour; one of our friends beckoned
to him, took him aside, and pulling out a revolver
("It is hands up!" thought Sir Henry), fully loaded,
pressed it on his acceptance in the kindest manner as a
useful *compagnon de voyage.* As we were not to stay
at Deming, the self-sacrifice was not consummated.

The regular train having come up, our special was
tacked on to it, and in an hour the locomotive puffed
out of the depot, and sped westerly on its way at the
rate of twenty miles an hour, across a plain some

fifteen miles broad, bordered by jagged, irregular mountain ranges north and south, as dry as a bone— so dry that water for the engine has to be brought to the stations in tanks. A scanty growth of what looked like camel grass, interspersed euphorbias and cactuses of great height, was all that met the eye. We are approaching the great basin of Arizona, and are warned that much dust and great heat must be expected, and that the " scenery " does not improve in point of variety or verdure, both of which are nearly at zero. A vigorous, well-directed campaign against the flies in the saloon gave us comparative repose; then the blinds being pulled down, and the thermometer reduced to 83 deg., society settled itself to study, with results indicated presently by a gentle *susurrus* on the sofas. A sudden alarm, " Look at the deer ! " There sure enough was a herd of antelopes flying over the scrub towards the horizon, which flickered about in the heat in a mirage of islands and uplifted mountain ends—so vanished.

After passing Lordsburgh, a desolate spot in the desert, there appeared a beautiful mirage. The sand became a sheet of water, waveless and mirror-like, and in it we saw reflected in trenchant outline the mountain range beyond. " It must be water! it is water ! " exclaimed an unbelieving director. And, lo! as he spoke the " dust devils " rose and danced along the face of the sea ; in another minute the vision was gone ; the dazzling sand, white, blank and dull, mocked our senses. This was near Stein's Pass, up which the train of nine carriages was climbing—" the heaviest train that has gone over yet," said the triumphant conductor. "But we thought we'd try it." Each waggon weighed 30 tons. The Pass is three miles long, and we were working at a grade of 74 feet with a 19-inch cylinder engine.

Between Pyramid Station and San Simon (*stant nomina umbrarum*—the names of mere shadows of stations) the western border of New Mexico is crossed, and we enter the great Territory of Arizona, which lies between the Rocky Mountains and the Sierra Nevada.

It is bounded by New Mexico on the east, by Mexico on the south, by Utah and Nevada on the north and north-west, and by California in continuation of the western boundary. It is as large as New York, Pennsylvania, Maryland, New Jersey, and Delaware together. Whom it belonged to first, so far as occupation constitutes possession, I know not; but the Spaniards owned and neglected it for more than three centuries before the Americans possessed it. In 1848 and 1853 the regions now forming Arizona, New Mexico, Colorado, Utah, and Nevada were ceded by the descendants of the Spanish conquerors to the conquering Anglo-American. It would need weeks of assiduous travel to explore the portion of Arizona where the most interesting ruins in America, the cities of the Zoltecs or the Aztecs—for the experts differ respecting their origin—are to be found. The weight of authority and of recent investigation leads one to believe that the Aztecs were not the builders

of these ruined cities. Humboldt, indeed, believed
that they were; but, as Mr. Hinton remarks, in
his capital little handbook, which I recommend to
prospectors, emigrants, tourists, and travellers, "to
suppose such an utter abandonment of settled habitations, it will be necessary to suppose some strange
impelling reasons, either in climate or other causes,
that must have amounted to a catastrophe. An
hypothesis which would leave a whole race able to
conquer an empire, and to preserve power enough to
abandon without destruction their old homes, implies
conditions and forces without a known historical
parallel." The conclusion that many native cities were
flourishing when the Spaniards arrived in America
may, perhaps, be questioned. There is a distinctive
character about them, differing from that of the
Mississippi mounds, the Central American pyramids, or
the ruined cities of Yucatan.

The site of one of these cities was pointed out to us
from the train, and that was all we saw of them.
But I heard so much about the mysterious remains
that I was induced to procure Mr. Bancroft's remarkable essay on the native races of the Pacific
Coast. Mr. Bancroft believes that the Pueblos and
other Indians, in a state of civilisation which they
subsequently lost, were the earliest inhabitants of these
countries and the builders of the cities; that the
Apaches came down upon them, and their work being
then aided by the Spaniards, this original agricultural
people were swept off the face of the earth. But

where the Apaches came from the American ethnologists have not, I believe, determined. For hundreds of miles these ruins cover the country—stone houses, ancient watch-towers, and adobe buildings, around which are quantities of stone implements, masses of crockery and pottery. In some places there are structures of wood and stone, without iron, the masonry consisting of thin plates of sandstone dressed on the edges, and laid in coarse mortar nearly as hard as the stone itself.

The explorers who have discovered the most interesting cities in Arizona and elsewhere were officers of the United States army. They have been the true pioneers of American civilisation in the West, and it is most creditable to them that they have been able to furnish so much scientific and antiquarian observation in the execution of their arduous and often painful duty in Indian warfare. There is no cold shade cast upon the labours of officers who desire to make a little reputation for themselves by contributions to scientific publications, and by papers on natural history and the like in periodical publications or in the daily press.

There is, as might be expected from its position, a very high temperature in Arizona. This lasts from the middle of June to the first of October. During the best part of summer exertion of any kind is impossible. Metal objects cannot be handled without producing blisters; rain scarcely ever falls; and, to keep up the drain of constant evaporation, a man must drink a gallon or two gallons of water a day. Mr. Ross Brown, speaking of the summer, declares that "everything dries. Waggons dry; men dry; chickens dry. There is no juice left in anything, living or dead, by the close of summer. Officers and soldiers creak as they walk; chickens hatched at the season come out of the shell ready cooked. Bacon is eaten with a spoon, and butter must stand in the sun an hour before the flies become dry enough for use. The Indians sit in the river with fresh mud on their heads, and, by dint of constant dipping and sprinkling, manage to keep from roasting, though they usually come out parboiled." But, although it is recorded that a party encamped on a narrow cañon where the temperature was 120 degrees, there was no sunstroke. And in that respect the climate differs from that on the eastern coast, where, especially this very summer, a great number of deaths were caused by *coup de soleil.* People, with the thermometer marking 94 degrees, talk of its being agreeably cold. An exceedingly interesting fact, if it be one, connected with residence in this part of the world is the wholesome effect of complete abstinence. Death from want of water was by no means infrequent in the old days before so many wells were dug; but it only occurs when there is a good deal of humidity in the air. Although alcoholic drinks and tobacco have an injurious effect, there is a large consumption of both at all the stations and at the mines.

As in the Orange River Free State, where probably

the conditions of temperature are not very dissimilar,
pulmonary complaints are cured, so a residence in
Arizona, it is said, stops consumption; and there
are authentic statements that people who arrived in
a rapid decline have experienced almost immediate
relief of the principal symptoms, and have been finally
cured. Governor Safford, in an official letter, states
that his lungs were a good deal diseased, and that he
was suffering with a severe cough when he reached
Arizona, and that in six months his cough left him.
He is satisfied the warm, dry atmosphere acted like a
healing balm to diseased lungs, and that, the pores
being kept open, the impurities which attack weak
organs escape through the skin. Dr. Loryea, of San
Francisco, and Dr. Sawyer aver that Arizona is
nature's Turkish bath, and that Yuma, that evil-look-
ing place, contains the fountains of health.

Of such vast regions a small acquaintance acquired
by passing rapidly twice over a line of railway does
not entitle one to speak; but, if what we read and
heard of Arizona be true, there is within its limits
enormous mineral and agricultural wealth. There
are carboniferous basins of great extent and richness.
The mountains teem with ore. Silver and gold, copper
pyrites, zinc, and lead are to be found over a great
range, the extent of which is as yet imperfectly
known. There are sulphates of nearly all the metals;
metallic oxides, chlorides, carbonates, nitrates; agates,
amethysts, garnets, and other precious stones. People
there are who believe that the diamond, the emerald,

and the ruby will turn up in due time. In fact, if one were to be guided by the accounts in the papers or the guide-books, he would think that a sure way of making an immediate fortune would be to settle down on any hillside in this favourite land. Nevertheless, what I saw out of my window gave me reason to suppose that there was poverty in Arizona as well as in the old country. Nor did the buildings which I saw by the way at the sparse stations and infrequent towns give an idea that the in-dwellers were well-to-do in the world. The adobe, or burnt brick, which is a common material in lieu of better, has always a ruinous appearance. The houses built of it yesterday seem tumbling to pieces from the influences of old age.

We take no note of time save by its relation to constant motion, and to the "programme"—a Procrustean bed on which we have voluntarily placed our tortured limbs. Sometimes in the hours of the night, which could not be called still because of the incessant pealing, rattling, and thundering of the train, I thought of the wonderful ways of man with himself in such affairs as we were now engaged in. There is a play of Terence which was a trouble to me in my youth, so long ago that I remember very little more of it than the dismal and elongated name; but Mr. "Heautontimórumenos" never needlessly bound himself up in a programme and delivered his life over to a time-table! It is likely enough, seeing what sort of man he was, that he would have adopted that course had he lived in these days.

I admit that programmes are necessary when your movements regulate, or have to be regulated by, those of other people ; and that was the case in some measure with us, but the solicitude it occasioned the worthy and valued friends, whose brows I perceived becoming more puckered, and whose faces and spirits were heavy with cares connected with the programme, to come up to time, was beyond belief, and I vowed if ever I had my own way with the ordering of a party I would have no programme at all. And plot and calculate as you will, a gale of wind, or a heated axle, or a broken bridge, or a flood, upsets everything, and your schemes gang aglee utterly ! It was admirable to see how we were working out the destiny we had made manifest for ourselves in advance so long ago, but the task was not easy. What curious sounds, by the way, our train made at night ! One could now and then compose words to the tune of the wheels, and the regular rhythm forced one at times to hum the words of a song, of which the train seemed to hammer out the music. It seemed so strange to be turning into bed night after night, and waking up to pass the same life day after day, like a log of wood carried on by an interminable, irresistible torrent.

Provided with books and newspapers, and friends to converse with, as well as with sights to see, we had, however, no reason to complain that time hung heavy on our hands as the train sped on. The books were very utilitarian, it is true—Reports of Chambers of Commerce, statistics and papers connected with railway and commercial enterprise and the like. But our directors took to that literature with avidity, and aided by maps and tables, copiously furnished to them, seemed bent on passing with honours in a competitive examination anent the American railway system. There were always, close at hand in the cars, competent authorities to answer questions, or able champions to engage in controversy, and as I heard all the subtle contentions, which I did not understand, concerning signalling and baggage checking, gauges and engines, curves and gradients, freights and fares, I was set to think what the field had been in which all the ingenuity and talent displayed in dealing with such topics were exercised in pre-railway days. These discussions were mostly connected with the consideration of profits and percentages, and that was a neutral ground on which the combatants manœuvred their facts and figures as in a natural *" schauplatz."* There were times when such investigations ran down like a clock, and no one wound them up again for a few hours, and then my friends digested the remains they found on the field of battle and strengthened themselves for friendly jousting.

Not very long ago there would have been exceedingly good sporting in many parts of Arizona. Grizzly bears, common and black bears ; pumas, mountain sheep, jaguars, ocelots, opossums, panthers, wolves, and lynxes are largely distributed over the hill ranges. There are also hares and rabbits and many smaller animals. Wild turkeys have much diminished of late years ; but there is a variety of birds, some of them

excellent for the spit. The chase, however, is attended
with some danger, unless one is very well booted and
looks out where he treads, as rattle-snakes abound, and
are of exceeding virulence, the black species being
especially deadly. There are horned toads, but these
are harmless.

For the botanist Arizona is an almost inexhaustible
field of delight. Any one who likes to read of vegetable wonders, or of an extraordinarily varied flora,
cannot do better than get Dr. Loryea's work, or read
' New Mexico,' by Elias Brevoort. The growth which
struck us most was that of the extraordinary cactus
called the candelabra or Sahuaro. It is worth while
going so far as the railway will take one to see these
plants sticking up on the sides of a rock without a
trace of verdure or moisture, rising to the height of
40 or 50 feet, and throwing out enormous arms at the
most grotesque angles, each varying from the other in
shape, the number of its arms, and in the manner in
which they are disposed. This giant cactus is covered
with prickles, and is of a light green colour. It is
said that in the old days the Apache Indians not unfre-
quently made use of them as handy means of torture,
and nailed their victims to a cactus previous to setting
fire to it. The body of the plant is resinous, and it
can be easily converted into a bonfire. Here and
there we saw some with traces of pale yellow flowers.
When these are gone there is a fruit, which makes an
excellent preserve, or can be boiled into sugar. Then
there are prickly pears in great quantities; and there

is a "negro-head cactus," with a round top covered
with sharp spines, which furnished the Mexicans with
fish-hooks. "There is a soul of beauty in things
evil." If a thirsty traveller coming upon one of these
plants kindles a fire around it, the juices of its body
are gradually concentrated into a central cavity, where
they only wait incision to be liberated in the form of
a pleasant drink, half a gallon or more in quantity.
The appliances for getting a drink out of most of
these roots are described at length in various books
of travel; but however useful they may have been at
the time, the activity of the Atchison, Topeka and
Santa Fé Railway will in all probability exempt
travellers in future from any necessity to avail themselves of these ingenious devices. Trees flourish in
spite of the heat and want of water. As various as
the trees are the human inhabitants, and one of
the greatest marvels connected with them, perhaps,
is the extraordinary variety of dialects amongst people
of the same race, who lived in the same country
long before the white man came to trouble them..
They are decreasing, of course, in numbers ; but in
some of the reservations they seem to have arrested
downward progress, and to have taken to some
form of agricultural labour. At present Arizona is
the happy hunting-ground of the unfortunate red
man. There is, I am assured, no disposition on the
part of the whites to intrude upon the reservations of
the various tribes. I did not hear of any one who

had come in from the East to settle with the view of making his fortune by farming; but miners have flooded the cañons, and climbed the mountain-tops; and now they have settled down into a steady way of life without any big "booms," as the Americans say, but with prospects of pretty certain returns for their labour.

All night we travelled on, and when the morning came, we were still traversing the desert, still passing through one of the most sterile wastes on the face of the earth, where, however, by strange contrasts of nature—or is it strange?—there were in the mountains and in the ravines rich ores to tempt the cupidity and enterprize of man. We are continually reminded of similar wastes in India and in Africa; but no one, as far as I know, has yet discovered any mineral wealth in the north-western deserts of our Indian Empire. And although Captain Burton and others have fancied they have come across an El Dorado in Southern Egypt, and Ibrahim Pasha had such faith in the existence of gold in those regions that he led forth an expedition to perish there, there is no such fortune in store for the adventurous miner as awaits him in Arizona, Colorado, and California.

June 1st.—Every one who has entered Arizona, or left it—and let us hope he went back all the better for his visit—will recollect Yuma for ever.

Yuma is on the Colorado, which divides California from Arizona. The muddy waters of the river rush with immense velocity past the buttresses of the fine bridge, with a draw for steamers, that spans it. The town consists apparently of adobe houses, and these not very regularly built. I could not visit the main street for lack of time, but the offshoots within eyeshot of us were not tempting. All we could see from the railway windows were flat-roofed adobe houses, some squalid Indians nearly naked, the buildings, with the Stars and Stripes over them, of the United States post on the left bank, and a few wooden sheds. It is said to be one of the hottest places in the world, and certainly looked dry and dusty. They say that a soldier who died there and went to an unmentionable place, returned in the spirit to beg for a blanket, as he felt so cold!

More happily constituted travellers than most of us have seen something pleasing in the aspect of the country roundabout, and have been moved to much admiration by the various tints of the hills in the distance, and by the rocks which constitute the near limits of the valley through which the river passes. In the old days, when the stage-coaches offered the only means of travelling through the district, there might have been a good deal to see along the road; but the rail generally avoids sights, and where nature is at its best, the engineer strikes deep down and burrows if he can. The colours of the hills are bright and varied; the lava rocks are of many shades, and the sun, piercing through stata of pure air, illuminates them with great vividness and force; but after a time the eye tires of the uniform hues of the landscape. For a few

miles the rail runs close to the river, then plunges
into the most remorseless, cruel waste of sand and
rock, spread out up to the foot of the rugged hills of
the Barnardino Range, I ever beheld—an abomination
of desolation compared with which the Libyan Desert
or the plains of Scinde were the Garden of the Hespe-
rides.   I cannot describe, nor could I at any time hope
to succeed in giving an adequate conception of this
dreadful wilderness.   For 107 miles west there is not
a drop of water to be found; the stations are de-
pendent on the railway for their supplies.   But
Nature, as if to take away the reproach of permitting
such a vast blotch on her fair face, kindly threw in
Fata Morgana.   We saw with delight widespread
lakes with fairy islands in the midst; placid seas
washing the base of the distant hills.   This baked and
dreary expanse extends nearly to San Gorgonio.   We
were spared the sandstorms which are so dreadful,
nor did we experience inconvenience from the dust.
The traveller, who has begun to despair of ever
seeing anything greener than giant cacti and the
adamantine vegetation which dispenses with water,
is agreeably surprised as he approaches Los Angeles.
If he be as fortunate as we were in having such friends
as Colonel Baker and his wife to take charge of him,
he will be amply repaid for far greater discomforts
than any he experienced in the Colorado desert.   From
Los Angeles there is a railway to Santa Monica, seventeen miles distant, which belongs to Colonel Baker;

and I would advise every one who can, either to spare
or make the time for a diversion to that most delightful spot. Judge of the pleasure we felt when, after a
picturesque run through orange groves, vineyards, and
fields of corn and barley, we gazed on the waters of
the Pacific—" θαλαττα! θαλαττα!" What a glorious
scene! the broad bay lighted by the rays of the de-
clining sun; the blue waves rolling on in solemn
march, and breaking in long lines of foam on the
dazzling sand, and nearer still the gardens and trees
of the Pacific Biarritz which was about to welcome
us! Our palace-car and its attendant carriages shot
into a siding close to the beach. In a few minutes
"every man Jack" was off to the bathing establishment to conform to the regulations ere we plunged
into the sea. It is an orthodox bathing-place of the
highest order. The Baths are extensive, and provided
with every convenience and comfort for ladies and invalids; hot and cold, salt water and fresh, for those
who do not like to trust themselves to the sea. A rope
extended seaward to hold on by was needful, for the
surf was heavy and the undertow strong. The water
was delicious. Generally there is less sea on, and it
is never too hot or too cold for bathing. Next morning
we had another bath in a still rougher Pacific. The
Duke and some of the party were driven about the
country by Colonel and Mrs. Baker, and at 3 p.m., to
our sorrow, we left the most lovable little spot of all
we have seen on this continent. Good fortune be in
store for Santa Monica! At Los Angeles, where car-

riages were waiting, we drove through the streets and
suburbs, which enabled us to appreciate the reasons
which induced the Spanish founders to give the city its
name.   In the evening we continued our journey,
passing in the dark over the feat of engineering called
the Loop.

CHAPTER II.

THE YOSEMITE VALLEY.

A new Land of Goshen—A Jehu indeed—The Drive to Clarke's
—A Mountain Hostelry—Grizzlies—Fascination Point—The
Merced—Yosemite Fall—A Salute—Mountain Airs—The Mirror
Lake—"See that Rattle?"—A Philosophic Barber.

June 2nd.—It is astonishing how soon one gets
accustomed to the rattle and rumble of the rail, and
sleeps all the night through after a time, waking up
only when a train stops at a station, just as a miller is
roused by the cessation of the clock of the mill-wheel.
We keep good hours, and so at 4.30 this morning I
was looking out of the window at a sea of blue mountain
ridges upon the west, which looked like the waves of
the ocean, so varied in the serrated edges was the line
of stony waves which seemed as if they were about to
sweep down over the great stretch of prairie. We
were passing through a new land of Goshen, at least
that was the name which I detected on the station
board, indicating a junction with another line, and early
as was the hour the door of the hospitable restaurant
was open, and gentlemen in front were to be seen
drawing their hands across their lips as if they had
been taking a refresher in the early morning. Close
at hand the country was perfectly flat, covered with

glorious crops nearly ripe for the sickle, and indeed cut and stacked in some places. Water appeared abundant; a river flowing west was visible at intervals, its course marked by a line of trees. Large black cranes stalked about in the meadow-like fields, and hares sat up on end to take a look at the train. The paucity of human beings, except at the rare stations, was remarkable; only when I say " rare," perhaps I am scarcely justified, as there were little wooden huts at intervals perhaps of ten or twelve miles, where a saloon announced itself, and a possible ticket-office.

On the east of the plain through which the line runs, the peaks of the Sierra Nevada were visible, but the journey was rather monotonous all the same, and we were glad when our train halted at Madera, about ninety miles from Goshen, where we were to get out and start on our expedition to the Yosemite Valley. Especial arrangements had been made for our conveyance, but I almost doubt now whether it would not have been better for us to have taken the ordinary carriage which leaves Madera every day, except Monday, for the Yosemite Valley, at 7.45, arriving at Clarke's or Bruce's in somewhat less than twelve hours, so as to bring daylight with it to the halting-place; a very desirable thing, as we soon found out. It was 8 o'clock before our party started from Madera, in two Kendal carriages with four horses each. In one was the Duke, Lady Green, Mr. Stephen, and myself, with Crockett on the box; in another were Sir Henry Green, Mr. Wright, Major Anderson, and Mr. Jerome.

Our driver was a man with the impossible name of
MacLenathan, a resolute, dry, taciturn man, with a
good face, seamed with the exposure to sun and rain of
many years on the box. But he told us he had deserted
it lately, and had taken to the work of livery stable
keeper, only coming out on this occasion as driver to
do honour to the Duke. As it turned out, it was well
his right and his left hand had not lost their cunning.
The driver of the other carriage was a noted character,
rejoicing in the name of " Buffalo Bill," and later on
we had reason to feel very thankful to him also for the
possession of great pluck and nerve. For some ten or
twelve miles the route, which consists of mere wheel
tracks over the prairie, runs over moderately undulating land. On the right there is a shoot or *flume* for
carrying down timber from the upper part of the
mountain ridge fifty miles away. The dust was
troublesome, and the rapid motion of the four horses
scarcely saved us from the roasting sun. The scenery
was not interesting; indeed, the great object of
attraction was the little Californian quail with his
pretty crest, running across through the grass or
jumping up upon a stump to have a look at the
travellers. Stage stables were far apart, but the
speed was fair, and it was astonishing to see the
excellent condition in which the horses were at
the end of their long canter, and what capital steeds
were taken out of the stalls, in which they were
feeding on barley-straw, to be put into the traces.
I think the average length of the stages was about

twelve miles. We lost about an hour at a little mining village where we halted for dinner, a place called Coarse Gold, as well as I recollect, consisting of the usual buildings, a few shanties, the store, the hotel, far better than might have been expected, and a sort of wigwam or one-storeyed house, in front of which were assembled a number of "Digger Indians," degraded specimens of a degraded tribe. They sat looking at the new arrivals in the most apathetic manner, just as they might regard so many flies. The men were dressed in a compromise of old Indian attire, leather leggings and deerskin jackets, with European clothing, caps, bad hats and trousers, and old boots, the women swathed ungracefully in what seemed to be pieces of blanket, their legs encased in folds of dirty cotton. One of these Diggers was very slightly dressed, and as it is intensely cold in the winter, we asked him whether he did not feel the effect of the frost and snow. He knew a little English, and made the most of it. "When your body is covered you do not feel the cold," he said; "But your face is always uncovered, and yet you do not feel the cold there. An Indian's body is all face." And that was all the explanation he would vouchsafe to us. Somehow or another, what with delays at the stations, possibly caused by our being out of the regular running, and being an interpolation on the ordinary course of travel, and possibly owing to our reduced speed, for the carriages with four horses did not, it seems, go as fast as the public conveyance with six, it was getting dark as we approached the line of wooded hills, in a valley in which, many miles away, lay our halting-place for the night. The result of our delay in starting, concerning which the driver had been severe from time to time, was startlingly manifest as the coaches mounted the steep ascents of one of the most tortuous roads in the world. The spurs of the hills come down very sharply to the valley, and the road is carried round by a series of very severe gradients following the contour of the mountain-chain, so that at one time there is a deep gorge on your left, and then, as the road leaves that spur with the valley on that side and crosses to another spur, there is a great descent on the right, so that you are continually passing along by a series of precipices, to which, in our case, the fast gathering gloom imparted additional horror. Through the sighing of the wind in the trees aloft came the roar of the torrents down below. The drivers went along at a good steady canter, and from time to time, as we came round a sharp curve, I dare say the thought was in every one's mind, what would happen if one of the leaders fell, or if the driver slipped his hand in gathering up the reins to go round the corner. The scenery became more wild and formidable, so to speak, at every fresh turn. The colossal trees, which challenged admiration in the daytime, closed up in greater volume, darkening the narrow road completely, so that in an hour after entering upon the mountain-range it became as black as pitch. The lamps of Buffalo Bill in the leading carriage were some guide to our driver. He had none, and it was with anxiety, renewed every ten minutes or so, that we saw the lights in front describe a graceful curve, which showed that they were passing by one of the dips or cuts of the road. It needed skill and judgment for MacLenathan to conduct the carriage, because if he drove too close to that in front of us, the clouds of dust obscured the view, and if he dropped too far behind he lost the benefit of the lights. By enormous trunks of trees, by piles of timber, through deep cuttings in the rock, plashing over watercourses, descending swiftly into river-beds, and splashing through the fords over boulders, then climbing up steep hillsides, on and on, it seemed as though the night would never come to an end, and we inwardly, and audibly too, expressed our regret that we had not started a little earlier; but still there was an almost pleasurable excitement in holding on as we swept round one of these terrible gorges, and tried to look down into the gulf beneath. That last stage seemed interminable, but towards 9 o'clock at night the driver of the coach in front announced that we were getting " near at last "; and lucky it was, for his lights were giving out. "It is just as well that they did not," said our driver, "because it would be bad for you." " Why ? " " Well," he said, " you would just have to get out and walk! I would not undertake to drive any one in the dark along such a road as this." Presently we heard the noise of rushing water, and gained the bank of a stream flowing with swiftness over a shingle bed. This we crossed, and in half an hour more, through the dark belt of trees in front, lights were discerned, and, crossing another stream and a bridge, our wearied horses were pulled up in front of the hotel, a large wooden building, on the steps of which were the landlord and his staff, and most of the inmates turned out to greet and inspect the travellers who had been long expected. "It is a bad country to go driving about in the dark," said Mr. Bruce, the landlord, a sentiment in which we thoroughly agreed. There was a supper in the common room, to which, albeit the fare was primitive enough, we did ample justice. Travellers have complained of the charges along the road, but, considering the distance which all articles have to be carried to the Valley, the heavy duties, and the shortness of the season, I do not think that any one with experience of Swiss inns would complain much; and if the traveller desires to drink claret, he must not be astonished if he pays eight or nine shillings a bottle for it. The ordinary fare, at hotel prices, is quite good enough for hungry people, and eggs, milk, and bread are abundant, and not dear. The bedrooms, sufficiently simple in all their appointments, are good enough to be welcome to tired people, for there is a fair bed to lie upon, and the sheets, as far as our experience went, were clean and fresh. Nor were the insect horrors, of which we may have some knowledge in parts of Europe, to be dreaded, not even mosquitoes at this time of year.

Soon after dawn a thunderstorm broke over the
valley, hail and torrents of rain, and the landlord con-
gratulated us upon the cooling effect it would have on
the air, and on the absence of dust, which is rather troublesome at times. It was necessary to make an early
start in the morning, for it is a long journey to the
Yosemite. For some years past the Valley has become a
kind of American Chamouni, and if Americans swarm
over Europe in search of the sublime and beautiful,
they cannot be accused of neglecting altogether their
own country. The first thing I saw, on walking out
on the verandah of the hotel, was the stage-coach and
six horses, with eight ladies and nine gentlemen,
loading up for the Valley. They had arrived late the
night before, a little in advance of us, and yet the
ladies, bravely attired for the road, were all in their
place in the *char à. bancs* long before 7. Travellers
frequently stay at Bruce's, and our host promises
good sport to any one who will make it his head-
quarters; but I cannot speak with any confidence on
that point myself; still I should think it a very pleasant quarter for a man who had nothing else to do,
and who had an aptitude for climbing, to go about
looking out big game. We heard talk of pheasants,
but saw none : the bird which is called by that name
not being entitled to it, according to ornithologists.
In front of the hotel was laid out the skin of
a cinnamon bear, which had been shot by an Austrian
gentleman—" Count Fritz Thumb," the landlord called
him—a few days previously, and which was to be sent

after him as a trophy of his skill. "But," says
Boniface, "it was not he shot him at all; it was 'is
old Injun hunter." Grizzlies, he said, were rare, but
they were to be found if you went up high enough,
and as he spoke he pointed up to the mountains
towering away in the distance in grand Alpine pro-
portions. Deer were common enough, and there were
some tame specimens of the ordinary black deer
running about in the enclosure. We had an early
start, but not quite so early as the Americans; and it
was wonderful how well our four hardy horses did
the first stage, six and twenty miles, including some
very sharp ascents from the Hotel.

From time to time we got out and walked up the
sharp bits, diverging to the right or left to gather the
lovely flowers which grew on the roadside, or halting
to admire the giant trees which clothed the mountain
ridges. Pitiable ignorance! not to know the names of
the plants or shrubs or wonderful bunches of blossoms,
among which fluttered the most magnificently coloured
butterflies. Woodpeckers of many different species
uttered their quaint notes in jerky flight from tree to
tree, or peered at the travellers from the shelter of the
branches. Firs, pines, and spruces of enormous size,
and trees to me unknown, formed a dense forest on
each side of the road; but now and then we caught
glimpses of the stupendous ranges of the alps beyond.
It was lamentable to see the waste and wreck wrought
in this wondrous wealth of timber—reckless, wicked
waste. Charred trunks stood with leafless arms

withered and black, or lay prone among the ferns in myriads. This was, we were told, the work of shepherds, who think nothing of setting fire to one of the finest trees in the world to warm themselves for an hour, and are delighted with a conflagration which may lay a hillside in ashes. And the Indians too are held to have their share in the destruction. There was enough of timber wasted and destroyed mile after mile to build a city. The nemesis must come; already the alarm has been sounded, and the State authorities here and elsewhere are trying to prevent the mischief. I have often had occasion to regret my ignorance of botany *inter alia ;* but never did I feel it more than when I was walking up the road, on each side of which was a carpet of flowers, a maze of shrubs and plants—dense brushwood—to not one of which could I give a name. We arrived at the Halfway House at 12.35 as much pleased as the horses which brought us there so well at the respite, for it was an awful " pull up," and the coachman did his work at high pressure. In the course of our pilgrimage we had found a very pleasant *divertissement.* The Major, Mr. White, and Mr. Jerome had excellent voices, and from time to time they burst into song, giving with great effect the quaint negro melodies, which are now made familiar to us in London, from a very large *répertoire ;* and so the afternoon passed in quiet enjoyment as we climbed the hills on foot or in the carriages—snatches of talk, exclamations of wonder and delight, and outbursts of the ' Golden Slipper,' ' O ! that 'Possum,' ' The

Ark,' 'John Brown,' 'Tramp, Tramp,' and other choruses.

It was near 4 o'clock when the driver, who had been silent for some time, looking round at us occasionally as one who would say, " Wait a little till I surprise you," suddenly pulling up, said, " Now, here you are. This is Fascination Point! Won't you get down a bit ? " And, lo! there indeed lay before us a scene of indescribable grandeur. I know nothing like the effect produced by Yosemite Valley when seen for the first time from this point. It has a characteristic which no other similar view I am acquainted with possesses. You take in at one glance stupendous mountain-ranges, all but perpendicular, beyond which you see the snowy crests of the great Sierra, the profound valley between them, a long vista of extraordinary magnificence, of cascades and precipitous waterfalls, and far down below a silvery river rushing through a forest composed of the noblest trees in the world, with patches of emerald-green sward and bright meadows.

I see that by a slip of the pen I have miscalled the place from which we got our first view of the wondrous scene. But I have a right to change the name for my own use. What the driver said was " Inspiration Point." I prefer my mistake, for the view inspires you with no feeling save that of wonder and delight. These sublime scenes appear to be beyond the reach of poetry. Niagara and the Yosemite have not yet found a laureate. The peculiar and unique feature of the

valley seems to me to be the height and boldness of
the cliffs which spring out from the mountain-sides
like sentinels to watch and ward over the secrets of
the gorge; next to that is the number and height of
the waterfalls; but it is only by degrees and by comparison that the mind takes in the fact that the cliffs
are not hundreds, but thousands of feet high—that
these bright, flashing, fleecy cataracts fall for thousands
of feet—that the rent which has been torn in the
heart of the mountains, till it is closed by the awful
granite portals beyond which no mortal may pass,
extends for miles. I thought as I gazed that it were
pity to descend, lest a nearer view might destroy the
effect of that *coup d'œil;* but the driver had regulated
the period for rapture. He whipped us up to our
places by word of mouth, and the carriages renewed
their course, now striking by bold zigzags down into
the valley for our destination, which was still six
miles away. I shall not attempt to describe my own
feelings, far less can I pretend to tell what others,
probably far more susceptible of the beauty and
grandeur of what we beheld than I am, may have felt
at the succession of the awe-inspiring revelations
of the tremendous grandeur of the Valley which came
upon us. What is the use of rolling off a catalogue of
names and figures?—even the brush of the painter,
charged with the truest colours and guided by the
finest hand and eye, could never do justice—that is,
could never give a just idea of these cliffs and waterfalls. "El Capitan! Oh, that's the name, is it?

Three thousand three hundred feet high!" And then you try to take in what that means. "And it's 3500 feet down to the Valley? Dear me!" "And that is the Cathedral Rock? And those two peaks are the Spires? I don't exactly see the resemblance; do you?"

There was a sort of wail of delight from us all as we came on the "Bridal Veil Fall"; and I do not think any one cared to know that it was just 60 short of 1000 feet high! Surely one of the most graceful, lovely *chutes d'eau* on earth, lost though it be from view behind the rocks at the close of its feathery flight! But there was no stopping to look at anything; relentless Fate drove us down and on, till the wheels rolled more evenly, and at last we came to the bed of the valley—some 1800 yards broad, opening out here and there yet wider—and we rejoiced in the sight of the bright clear water of the Merced, child of innumerable icy mothers, flashing, sparkling, dashing and brawling, like a myriad Lodores, between her banks decked with flowers and covered with forest trees.

Suddenly there dashed out of a glade two cavaliers, and made full tilt at the leading carriage. "To arms!" Not a bit of it! Nor banditti or Injuns— of whom we had met one or two riding sullenly along to the hunting-grounds—no, only two hotel touts armed with cards of self-commendation, and not apparently in much rivalry, for when told that we had engaged our hotel, they galloped off to waylay other travellers, of whose coming they were apprized by our driver. Our hotel, I may say by the way, gave us full contentment. The site was admirable, commanding a full and near view of *the* Fall of Falls—the Yosemite—which had so fascinated our eyes that we could scarce divert them to any other object—not " Widow's Tears," or " Virgin's Tears," nor the "Three Brothers," not anything but the Yosemite! And so, when our rooms were pointed out, we made off to the spot where the fine cloudlike vapour rising above the tree-tops indicated the basin into which the waters sought rest after their troubled leap.

Our way lay through the usual gathering of stores, hotels, livery stables for the horses and ponies needed for the excursions, and curiosity dealers' shops, to the village street, as it may be termed, shadowed by fine trees, under which reposed some Indians—one of whom, an Amazon in yellow toga, went riding full gallop past us, her hair falling in a black mat on her shoulders, sitting low, in Melton style, regardless of poultry, children, and boulders, and vanishing in a cloud of dust under the trees. Then we turned to the left and crossed the river by a rustic bridge ; and as I looked down into the dancing waters certain shadow-like objects flew up against the current. " Trout ? " asked I. " Yes, they're trout. They take 'em—when they dew—five pounds weight. The Injuns catch 'em. We don't understand it as well." A short walk, with eyes ever up-turned, and we come out to a moraine, and, clambering up over a mass of trunks of trees and decaying timber, *the* Falls were before us— I cannot write more—no adjective will do. "Two thousand six hundred and thirty-four feet, mind!" says the voice. "I don't care," thought we, "it's the most beautiful and wonderful water-jump ever seen by human eye." "It only remains," as they say, to state that there is first, falling over a sheet of granite straight as a wall, a considerable river, which in the plunge [comes down at once 1600 feet. There, in a basin of rock, it collects its scattered forces, under cover of eternal spray and cloud, and then takes another header of 434 feet to a barrier of granite, against which it rages for a mad moment, till it swells over and escapes from control by another spring of 600 feet sheer down—and now it is free, and rushes past at our feet, a joyous flashing stream.

We returned through the meadows from the Falls, and as I was walking in advance of the party a snake wriggled across the path, which I struck at instinctively with my stick, and was lucky enough to kill at the first blow. I exhibited the carcass, or whatever a snake's dead body may be, in triumph to my companions. Further on our way we fell in with an old Frenchman who was carrying a basket of fruit from his little garden to the inn. With all the courtesy of his country, he offered to Lady Green the choicest in his little *corbeille*. He came from Lorraine very long ago to prospect in the States, almost the earliest of the pioneers, but he was still strong and active, and he pointed with great satisfaction up to a white flag planted on a dizzy height above, which he said he had placed with his own hands. The chief livery stable keeper is a German named Stegman. The first ascent of the Dome was made by a young Scotchman named Anderson, from Montrose; so with Indians, Americans, Mexicans, Europeans, there is a very liberal representation of the nations of the world, in the season, in the valley. Mr. Hutchinson, the Conservator of the Valley—one with all the enthusiasm of the American character in everything pertaining to the country, aggravated in this instance by an intense admiration for the valley over which he is appointed to watch—joined us at dinner in the little inn. Full of information, bubbling over with anecdote and illustration, and replete with all kinds of knowledge concentrated upon the one object—the Valley—the Valley—and nothing but the Valley. He knows its history since the time it was first discovered, and its natural history and geological formation, and all about the Indians who lived there and their traditions. It so happened that the Commissioners of the State of California, who are bound to visit the public domains, were also at the hotel, and so we had quite an unofficial and ceremonious meeting; and presently, as we stood in front of the hotel gazing up on the peaks, lighted up by the stars, and listening to the thunder of the waterfall, a startling report burst out on the night, and in another instant the echoes repeated from rock to rock were crashing through the Valley with the roar of heaven's artillery. It was the first gun of a salute ordered by the Commissioners to be fired in honour of the Duke's arrival. The effect was very fine, but I doubt whether I did not feel full of resentment at the outburst, very much as the owls and night-hawks might have been expected to feel, if one could judge from their cries. However, even a salute and echoes must come to an end, and as we were to get up early to start for the Mirror Lake, we turned in to bed at an early hour; not, however, to sleep, because the indefatigable and numerous company in the public room, off which were our bedrooms, were in high spirits, and the song and the dance, to the accompaniment of an invalid piano, for some time asserted their sway.

Mr. Hutchinson had the Duke out early, because it is one of the obligations to see the sun rise, reflected in the Mirror Lake—if you can. There is no fear of cloud or rain. In the Mirror Lake is reflected—or was as we saw it—the precipice at the other side of the Valley, the bulk of Mount Watkins (so called from a photographer who has been daring and successful in his renderings of the Yosemite), and all the surrounding scenery. Once a friend and I saw a cow on its back in the air, by the shore of a Highland lake. The surface was smooth as that of the Mirror before us now. It was flapping its tail from side to side, and its forelegs were up in the sky. We could not make it out at first. There was, in fact, a cow standing near the water of the loch; and what we saw was a reflection of the animal, actually stronger and better defined than the object itself. So it was with the reflections in the Mirror Lake; but when the sun rose over the cliff and we looked at the water, the glare was too dazzling. "It was," as Mr. Wright remarked, "like the electric light." There were curious optical effects produced, some being troubled with purple, others with green or yellow in their eyes, after a vain attempt to look at the reflection, but that did not last long.

We returned to breakfast to make an early start for Union and Glacier Points on ponies. Among the company at the hotel, introduced by Mr. Hutchinson, there was a young lady who was well acquainted with the Valley, and who proved to be a very agreeable companion in our mountain ride; but it was not long ere she was candid enough to let it be known that she did not visit the Yosemite out of love of the picturesque and beautiful, but that she was interested in the sale of photographs of the Valley, and was, in fact, a very persuasive and efficient agent of a firm in San Francisco, who had thus established an outlying picket of great activity and vigilance; and I am sure we all hope she may always be as successful with the visitors as she was with us. Of what we saw from the Glacier Point I must leave others to write or speak. It is reached by a zigzag on the mountain-side—a peculium of the maker, and all the "trails," as they are called, in the valley are the property of individuals or firms who are paid by tariff, and we heard "Eleven

gone up before—Duke Sutherland, Lady Green, Sir
Green, Mr. Wright, Mr. Russell, Mr. Jerome coming!
Sixteen coming up behind!" On the plateau behind
the cliffs, from which you look down on the Valley and
at the snowfields on the mountain ranges opposite,
there is a log house and shanty, and there we had
a mountain meal ere we began the descent.

Nothing in the way of riding is more disagreeable
than going down a very· sharp mountain-side on a
pony not, for all you know, very sure-footed, and so
instead of riding, I resolved to walk, now and then
taking a short cut, to the great discomfiture of feet
and boots, although it is three thousand feet to the
bottom, and make the best of my way and the
most of the road, which is very fair, down the zigzags. I reached the plain thoroughly hot and tired,
and bathed in perspiration, in fifty-seven minutes.
The horsekeeper, who came down with the rest of
the party, seemed to have been affected by the
rarity of the atmosphere or something else up at the
mountain hostelry, for he insisted on it that I had
ridden down, and demanded his horse. "What the
thunder, Russell, have you done with my horse?" he
asked again and again. Satisfied for the time by my
assurances that I had not ridden at all, he went off, and
then, thinking over the matter, came back again to
repeat his question, till I told him I would not answer
it any more. He was an amusing fellow in his way,
and affable. He called the Duke "Sutherland," now
and then putting Mr. before it. As he was watering

his horses, he said: "Here, Mister Sutherland, lay
hold of the bucket, will you, whilst I take a turn at
this one." And the Duke did so with alacrity. It was
a day of incessant activity. No sooner had the mountain party come down than they were off again to drive
through the Valley. The rest of our party had already
executed masterly investigations at the foot of all the
waterfalls; admired the Bridal Veil and the Widow's
Tear, as one cascade is satirically termed, "because,"
says the guide, "it dries up in six months;" had
driven and ridden everywhere and seen everything,
and we had to do the same; but it would need a week
of conscientious work to exploit the Valley thoroughly.
At half-past 7, the dinner hour, the little inn was
swarming with people; the stage had arrived with
fresh contingents. Every place was full, and what
with the clatter of knives and forks, the clamour of
waiters, the tumult of voices laughing and talking, it
was scarcely possible to conceive that a few short years
ago this valley was in the exclusive possession of the
Indian and the wild beast. There is now, however, a
great conflict of interests, and Mammon is holding his
revels in the Valley. The State has voted a certain
sum of money, twenty-five thousand dollars, I think, to
buy up the interests of the trail-makers; that is, those
who struck out and made paths to the various objects
of attraction; but no success has yet been attained
in the negotiations, and, indeed, I should think it
a very bad investment for most of them to accept
their share of such a sum. Macaulay, for example,

who made the path up to the point from which we descended to-day, must make many hundreds of dollars in the height of the season, as he charges so much a visitor, and, besides, has a restaurant where they take their meals at the top.

Next day (June 5th) we left the Yosemite with the satisfactory assurance that we had made the most of our time, though we could not believe we had done it justice. There were some small " nuages " on the face of our " Mirror Lake," caused by changes in the mode of conveyance; but we found six horses and one of the coaches of the country were better than four horses and two carriages of less capacity. Yosemite, I may tell my readers, means " Grizzly Bear " (it may be " Great Grizzly Bear "); but we only heard of one having been thereabouts for a long time, and I believe it was thoroughly tamed. After a glorious day in the woods, clambering up the steep from the Valley, and then on by the road—the only one—to Clarke's, halted there for the night, when we returned from a ceremonious visit to the " Big Trees." We had a most delightful ride from Bruce's, and a hard canter back through the woods on capital ponies, full of life and action, and very sure-footed, but rather inclined to have their own way, which was not always that of the rider. We turned into bed at Bruce's, quite delighted with our expedition, and rather anxious to see the road we had traversed in the dark by the garish light of day. Every traveller's tale, and every guide-book of recent date relating to this part of the world, has a full

account of the dimensions, number, appearance, and
condition of these wonders of the world. They are either
prostrate, mutilated, or decaying ; not one has survived
the stormy life he must have led for some 3000 years—
a few hundreds more or less do not signify. Those
which remain upright are scarred by fire and lightning,
and drop their monster arms, hung with ragged foliage
and. sheets of bright moss, mournfully over the ground
where their trunks will repose in time to come.
I cannot conceive any object of the kind so magnificent
as one of those Washingtonias in the full vigour of
mature treehood ; but we could only fancy what it
must have been like by measuring the stems, for there
was not anywhere in the forest a tree to be seen which
had not suffered. The best way to visit the scene—
for it may well be called so—is to strike out from the
road on the way to the Yosemite before the halt at
Bruce's ; but the hotel-keepers and stage-drivers will
persuade the stranger, if they can, to defer the
excursion till his return from the Valley, so as to make
a half-day more out of him.

June 6th.—All up at 5 o'clock, and off soon after
6 A.M. The first stage, eleven miles, we did in two
hours and ten minutes—a very pretty road ; the
second stage, eight miles, in forty-four minutes. The
ravages made by fires are most deplorable. We had
passed through this great forest track in the dark, but
now seen in the morning light, the trunks of magnificent trees rotting on the ground, or standing upright
with lifeless arms. consumed at the base, were visible

everywhere. It is difficult to find out the exact truth
about the cause of these fires. Some few people said
" it was the Indians," but the weight of testimony attri-
butes them to the shepherds, who for the most trifling
purposes kindle a great fire. In some of the large
trees they have hollowed out regular chambers, and of
course the tree dies. Such waste of timber ! For
mile after mile we passed scenes of desolation which
ere long those who allowed them will have cause to
regret. From time to time we encountered on the
road trains of waggons drawn by teams of handsome
mules with bells, and had occasion to admire the
economy of labour exhibited in the management, by
which the driver is enabled to work a powerful break
with one hand whilst he drives with the other. The
next stage, of fourteen miles, was over an exceedingly
bad road ; but the horses were good, and we rattled
along at a capital speed down towards the plain. Once
the quick-eyed driver, pulling up suddenly, said, " See
that rattle ? " leaped down and made towards the
bush ; and as we followed him, sure enough we heard
distinctly the noise of the snake, which he had inter-
cepted on its way to a rabbit hole. It took refuge in
a clump of bushes with gnarled roots, and coiled itself
round one of the branches ; but by a course of judicious
and rather nervous poking it was driven from its
vantage ground, and trying to escape was killed by
the driver with a blow of his whip, followed by a good
many unnecessary strokes from the rest of the party.
It was over three feet long, and had just been making

an evening meal upon a rabbit, which it had left where we had startled it; and it was evident from its swollen appearance that it had been for some time engaged in the warren close at hand.

At 10.20 we reached Presno, which is what the Americans call "quite a place," containing not only an hotel, a restaurant, and a store, but a shop where photographs were exhibited. The *chef-d'œuvre*, a portrait of a Spanish lady 140 years of age, living at Los Angeles, did not, however, commend itself to our taste. We halted at Coarse Gold at 11.40, and left at 12.35. Mr. Jerry Loghlan—who excused himself for not working on the ground that "there was no use in it, as there was nothing to be had," the mines being worked "out"—whose acquaintance we had made on the way up, a huge, broad-shouldered *vaurien*, was still hanging about with his specimens of quartz, gold, and rattlesnakes' tails, and a black eye recently acquired in battle.

After a long, hot, and dusty drive, it was with no small gratification we made out on the flat the houses of Madera, and after a time the carriages of the special train. The air is so bright and pure that the distances are very deceptive, and it was nearly 5 o'clock P.M. before we reached the station, which had been visible for more than an hour previously. It was pleasant news to hear that the little German barber at the way-side had got baths all ready. In the rear of his shop there was a row of apartments, each provided with a clean zinc bath, hot and cold water to turn on at discretion, and an abundance of towels. This in the centre of a waste seemed very creditable to the civilisation of the people. I should like to know in what part of Europe you would get similar comfort under similar circumstances. I am afraid there are many parts of the British Islands where a traveller would demand such a luxury in vain. And the barber was there to shave those who needed it, and to give you all the news of the day if you wanted it. He was a Prussian, and he grinned from ear to ear as, in reply to my question whether he had served, he said : " Serve, indeed ! Not I. I came away and escaped from all that nonsense. There is not a king or an emperor or a prince that I would fight for. Why should I ? " " But," said I, " you would have to fight for the Republic here if it were in danger; and that would not be fighting for your fatherland." " Yes," said he, " it would, for this is my fatherland now. But I do not want to fight for it either if I can help it. Fighting is nonsense."

Our excellent stewards received us, if not with open arms, with smiling faces. The carriages were trim and clean and fresh, the tables spread out, and all kinds of dainties provided for the evening meal. We rested quietly for the night in the siding at Madera, and got under weigh at 5 o'clock on the morning of June 7th, the train being timed so as to reach San Francisco at 12.30.

CHAPTER III.

SAN FRANCISCO.

The Palace Hotel—General McDowell—Palo-Alto—The " Hcod-lums "—The Real Sir Roger—Exiles in the Far West—The Chinese Population—For and Against them—The Sand Lot—Fast Trotters—The Sea Lions—The Diamond Palace—The Coloured Population—" Eastward Ho ! "

THE British Consul, Mr. Booker, who has been watching over the interests of the Queen's subjects for some thirty years here, and who is an institution by himself, met the train at a place called, I think, Porta Costa, and welcomed the Duke and his friends. There had been for some days an infusion of the Chinaman in the general element of life along the line, but here it became concentrated, and then ceased to attract much attention. As the train approached the wide expanse of muddy water from the Sacramento, which charges down with impetuous volume, and colours the bay with its turbid stream, we could form an idea of some of the advantages in the expanse of navigable river, that had, however, lain long without appreciation but for the bright red gold possessed by San Francisco. The bay is animated; white canvassed craft stud its waters, and the smoke of steamers pollutes the clear, bracing air. Italian fishermen are busy with line and net, and flights of ducks and squadrons of gulls and cormorants show that the waters are well stocked. It was too late in the year to see the country in the full affluence of its wealth of fruit and crops, of hay and corn, and the hillsides and fields are now disappointingly brown. Presently we arrived at Oakland, where the train was run out on a pier 3500 yards long, to the steam ferry-boat which was to convey us across to San Francisco. The ferry-boat was crowded, for Oakland is a city of some 50,000 people; and of course it had once on a time, not very remote, only a few sheds and insignificant houses. From this side of the bay the city of the Golden Gate, some miles away, was now visible in all its pride of place—pride but not beauty, now at least —for the city presents no great attraction to the eye. The streets, running in parallel lines at right angles to the quay right up the sandy hillside, look like the ribs of some stranded monster, " lank and lean and brown." The most prominent object is the hotel to which we are going, which towers far over the general level of house-top, steeple, and factory-chimney.

There is a little pamphlet, crammed with statistics and with an array of figures and superlatives enough to daze one, given to the guests of the Palace Hotel ; but those who are in that happy category scarcely need the information, and those who are not could not derive any idea of the building from the repetition of the ciphers which are to be found in the guide-book. The drawing on the outside affords the best notion of the size, but only actual purview can enable one to judge of the excellent arrangements, the service, the table. For once the American idol "Immensity" is not overlaid. "'Tis blinding bright — 'tis blazing white! O Vulcan! what a glow!" Electric lights flooding the court with brightness beyond description. And what a court! Sweetness and light indeed! In the great quadrangle, 144 feet by 84, there are fountains playing, groups of statuary, and exotic plants, and, tier after tier, rise the pillared terraces outside the seven storeys of which the main building consists, painted a lustrous white, shining like purest Parian. There are 755 rooms, abounding in conveniences, and comfortably luxurious. Each is provided with high-pressure hot and cold water, and there is an elaborate system of ventilation, alarms, conductors, pneumatic tubes, telephones, and "annunciators" for fire, letters, servants, &c. The beds are excellent; the furniture admirable; and this vast structure, 120 feet high, 275 feet broad, and 350 feet deep, is not only fire, but—listen—"earthquake proof"; so says the bill of fare, and so says ex-Senator W. Sharon, the proprietor. I have not the least desire to test the truth of the averment, but if I must be in a hotel when an earthquake visits the city in which I am, let me be in the Palace, San Francisco. A man may live here in the enjoyment of a pretty continuous series of meals and one of the best bedrooms for four dollars a day, and there is a lower tariff of bed and board at three dollars a day.

June 8th.—Our first day was rendered exceedingly

pleasant by the kindness of General McDowell. The weather did its very best to prevent our enjoying it, and was signally defeated. San Francisco is perhaps the windiest city in the world, and at this time of year there is almost always a storm in the harbour, and a steady, powerful, and somewhat chilly blast, setting in a little before noon, and lasting throughout the day until nearly sundown, up the streets. The General's aide-de-camps came over early to the hotel, in full uniform, in honour of Major-General Green, but General McDowell appeared in mufti, which eased us down a little. A powerful steamer, the "*General Macpherson,*" was prepared for the party, which was swollen by a considerable number of gentlemen invited by our host to meet the Duke, and the gentlemen from Topeka, who were included in the invitation. The excursion afforded a favourable opportunity of inspecting the city defences. From Alcatroz Fort, Point and Presidio Island batteries, which would not be considered very formidable as far as armament is concerned, although their position affords great advantages for torpedo defence, salutes were fired in honour of Sir Henry Green. But in the case of some of us the sight was marred by the rising sea, which increased to an inconvenient height as the steamer reached the Seal Rocks, close to the entrance to the bay. Of the seals I shall give an account farther on. They did not seem to mind the steamer very much until she blew her whistle, when many of them splashed into the sea. At the termination

of the trip, which lasted some four hours, General
McDowell entertained the party at his official quarters,
which are beautifully situated on a bluff overhanging
the water of the bay.

June 9th.—We spent, in some respects, an abortive
and deceitful day; not, indeed, that there was anything
disappointing about our entertainment at Belmont,
under the auspices of ex-Senator Sharon; but that
we started full of enterprise, and intent upon inspecting
the great works of the Spring Valley Reservoir, and of
making an excursion through what was described as a
very beautiful county whence is brought the water
supply of the great city in which we were sojourning.
However, though we were baulked in the object of our
expedition, the day passed, and not in the least degree
unpleasantly, and instead of going to the Lakes we
drove about the neighbourhood of Belmont, and visited
several country seats.

No one who visits San Francisco should omit taking
an early opportunity of going to Palo-Alto to inspect
the stock of General Stanford's thorough-breds, and the
breeding establishment, which as a sample of perfect
order and management cannot be surpassed. I cannot
answer for the figures, but I was informed that the
owner spends 25,000*l.* a year upon the maintenance of
his stud and stables, and that he has not as yet sold a
colt or filly, or parted with a single animal; sires,
mares, and young brood now amounting to about 700
head. They are beautifully housed in detached stables
fitted up with every convenience that a horse of the

highest pedigree and most luxurious taste can desire. I was particularly struck with the perfect silence which prevailed throughout the stables. No shouts to "stand over there," and none of that "——" (groom's expletive) which is so common in our country. And partly owing perhaps to that mode of treatment, and to gentleness in handling, all the horses without exception seemed tractable and sweet-tempered. High-bred stallions stood out in the open for our inspection, and allowed themselves to be rubbed and felt without even laying down their ears or raising a hind-leg from the ground. In reply to a question respecting a remarkably beautiful animal, which seemed to have a little more fire in him, the head groom said "You may walk under his belly if you like," and then and there he told one of the grooms to do so, which the man did, without attracting any unusual degree of attention from the animal. Outside one of the large blocks of stables there is a kind of testing arena, in which we were told it was the pleasure of General Stanford, when he was at home, to sit watching the performance of his young horses. It is an ellipse, like a large circus, bordered with a hoarding, and in the centre there is a raised stage for the visitors, on which are revolving chairs. The riding-master, with an attendant, performing the functions of the late Mr. Widdicombe, sets the animal in motion, checking him when he breaks into a gallop. The speed at which the animal trots the ellipse is known by the time marked on a chronometer, and the fact is recorded for the information of the inspectors,

who can turn round their chairs and follow the action
of the horse as it trots round the ring.

The district of the State in which Palo-Alto is
situated boasts of several residences of the Californian
millionaires. One house which we visited, I think
belonging to Mr. Flood, furnished the most ornate and
beautiful examples of woodwork that were ever seen
by any of the party. The house, which was as large
as a good-sized English country mansion, is constructed
of timber of the finest quality, beautifully worked,
painted and varnished; and with moderate care a mansion of this kind will last, in this climate, a couple of
hundred years, which to the American mind is an
eternity. There were artists from New York, and the
staff of an upholsterer and decorator of great renown
from the Empire City were still busily engaged in the
place as we went through the rooms. The magnificent
halls, reception-rooms, billiard-rooms, library, bedrooms, all fitted up with extraordinary luxuriousness,
but in a somewhat florid taste, were of wood, the doors
of many of the apartments arresting attention by their
extraordinary beauty and finish. The ceilings decorated
in fresco by Italian artists, and bright windows filled
with stained glass gave an appearance of light and
grace to the whole residence. The kitchen arrangements
were marvels of ingenuity, and one envied the butler
who would have such a pantry as that which was displayed for our inspection. Some of the pictures which
were ready to be placed on the walls were remarkable,
however, only for the richness of their frames; and,

indeed, we heard that the excellent proprietor was not a man of very cultivated taste; a child of fortune, in the prime of life and of money-making, spending a portion of his enormous wealth with an easy hand, but destitute of what is called book-learning, and leaving to some future generation the cultivation of the graces and the acquirement of accomplishments which the circumstances of his early life had denied him to effect.

It had been arranged that we should return to San Francisco to dinner, but Senator Sharon had in his secret heart resolved that we should do nothing of the kind, or at least, that if we did so, it should only be after we had partaken of such a feast at Belmont as would very much indispose us to test the capabilities of the *chef* of the Palace Hotel. From Palo-Alto accordingly we were driven to the charming country house, some miles away, of the ex-senator of Oregon, and we were regaled there, after some delay, at a very elaborate *déjeûner*, sent out from San Francisco. It was nigh 8 o'clock ere we got back to the city; and the night ended by what might well be called "an excursion" to the Baldwin Theatre, which was at the time the most attractive of the places of entertainment of that sort open in the city. As some of us were walking back, after the play was over, with an American friend, talking of the "hoodlums," famous rowdies, who, we were assured, had been of late days utterly broken up by the vigilance of the police, our attention was attracted to a number of lads smoking at the corner of the street. Our friend said "Hoodlums broken up! There they

E 2

are—don't you believe it. That's a lot of them, and if you were alone you might find out very unpleasantly that there are plenty of them."

The San Francisco journalists possess astonishing powers of imagination. I rubbed my eyes when I read that I had described "with eloquence the similarity between a marsh at San Bruno and a patch of jungle in the north-west of Scinde, where I had the felicity of spending three weeks with General Green while the natives were arranging a plan to capture the party and cut our throats." I never was in the north-west of Scinde in my life, and, although I had the pleasure of passing a longer time in his company in the United States, and of being on the same plateau before Sebastopol when he was there, for a still longer period, many years before, I never spent three weeks there with General Green. The Duke was described as "professing, but showing, little enthusiasm." However, these matters are of very slight interest or importance; only one wonders how many of the readers of this sort of literary work believe in it. One of our party has, according to a local paper, become a clergyman, and now rejoices in the style and title of "the Bishop," by which he is universally addressed by the party.

While in the train, on our way to Belmont, I had the pleasure of being introduced to a gentleman who, although a lawyer in very large practice, is General of the State Volunteers; and in the course of conversation, I heard that he had papers containing

the statement of a gentleman who had visited, and
which convinced him that the real Roger Tichborne
was living not very far from San Francisco. General
Barnes, whose name and character stand high in the
city of the Golden Gate, and whom I found to be a
gentleman of great intelligence, seemed perfectly
satisfied by the story told by this new "claimant";
but what he mentioned to me did not at all tend
to create in my mind any notion that he was not an
impostor, and especially were my doubts confirmed by
the quotations which General Barnes made from some
of the narrative, in which there was a ridiculous jumble
of French and English, in order to justify, apparently,
the stress placed by the "claimant" in his story on
that part of his life which was passed in France. He
spoke of his uncle as "mon oncle," and of Thursday as
"Jeudi," and so on. However, General Barnes appeared
to be so impressed by the truthfulness of the man's
bearing, and by the full details he gave him at an
audience in which he supplied the facts for the
consecutive narrative which I was promised, that I
expressed a desire to read it. General Barnes subsequently sent me a long written paper containing the
heads of the claimant's story, a perusal of which
strengthened the conviction I had previously entertained. I only mention this circumstance because
there was a report spread throughout the Press, by the
agency of one of the great telegraphic associations
which furnish the American public with intelligence,
that the Duke of Sutherland and myself had inter-

viewed the real Roger Tichborne at San Francisco, and had satisfied ourselves that he was the man; and innumerable "headings" were invented for this supposed interview, of which I was soon made aware on my return westward in every newspaper that I read. I promptly denied the statement that the Duke or myself had seen the new claimant, and although the denial appeared in print I was exasperated day after day by being asked questions afterwards with regard to this supposed conversation with Tichborne at San Francisco, and by inquiries as to my real impression; so it would appear that no one had seen or paid any attention to the refutation of the story which had brought down on my devoted head communications from friends of other Tichbornes, of whom there are several living, some in poverty and others in comparative affluence, in various cities and districts of the United States. I had further the mortification of seeing it stated in print that I had used disparaging words in alluding to the credulity of General Barnes, which was an entirely baseless fabrication. With all the extraordinary keenness of the American mind generally, there is associated with it a considerable amount of the Anglo-Saxon quality which is termed "gullibility," and the land swarms with impostors who make a living out of the easy faith of the population. I do not speak merely of spiritualists, quacks, and professors of peculiar religions or medical dogmas, nor of the preachers of eccentric forms of faith or unbelief, but of the mass of persons who contrive to get an existence by

representing that they are "someone else." Although
their tricks are well known, the trade still flourishes.
They are always the "sons of peers," who have got
into disgrace with their families, but who will eventually
be owners of castles of historic fame and of enormous
estates; "distinguished soldiers"; "Maids of Honour
to the Queen," who for some unknown reasons are
living in small out-of-the-way villages in the West;
or political conspirators who have played a great part
on some distinguished stage and have saved themselves from the consequences of defeated enterprize by
taking refuge in the States. And then there are
hordes of persons who are known by the title of "confidence men," who travel about on the trains or in the
steamers, looking out for victims, or lounging about
the bars and saloons, waiting for their prey in the shape
of some facile and easy-eared stranger, who in consideration of their merits and distress shall give them
temporary assistance. Sometimes, doubtless, there are
cases of very real suffering, sorrow, and poverty, to
which exile in the United States affords a melancholy
refuge. I was obliged to hear in one great city of a
gallant soldier who, reduced to poverty by no fault of
his own, had quitted England and given up the
society of his friends, and lived in a small suburb of
a town on the coast of the Pacific, his secret known
only to one or two officials, shunning all contact with
his countrymen and evading as far as possible all
inquiries of his friends. In San Francisco, where
there is a poor-house open to strangers and to native-

born Americans alike, there are, I am told, to be met with extraordinary exemplifications of the "downs" of fortune. Adventurous and daring spirits, and pioneers of civilisation, at one time probably possessed of wealth which was wasted in dissipation, or lost in unfortunate speculations, are there, talking of the days that are gone, in all languages of the world, and awaiting their end; while others who started with them in the same race are building their palaces or revelling in the enjoyment of wealth, compared to which our greatest fortunes are, if figures can be trusted, a mere bagatelle. How rapidly some of these fortunes can be made was illustrated by numerous stories connected with some of the richest men in California. I was told by an eminent tradesman of San Francisco that one day a miner came into his establishment to buy a watch, which he said must be cheap and good, for he wanted something he could trust to in the matter of time, as he was going off with a party on an exploring expedition after gold. This was in the early time of the great "booms" in the West. He selected a watch, for which he paid $40, and departed. The following day he appeared in the shop and asked to see the proprietor, and then, producing the watch, he said he would like to have $30 for it, as he had lost all his money in a "spree" the night before and must have something to start with. The jeweller said, "Well, I will return you what you gave me for the watch, as it has suffered no harm, and you shall have your $40 back again." The man went away exceedingly rejoiced, and the incident was forgotten. Some eighteen months afterwards a man came to the establishment, and looking at rings, gold chains, and jewellery of the most costly character, and asking for the best of everything that they had got, gave orders which occasioned the attendant to have some doubts as to his sanity, or certainly as to the means he had of paying the amount, which was rapidly running up to tens of thousands of dollars. So he sought out his principal. The strange customer said, "I suppose you don't know me?" which was admitted to be the case. He went on buying all the same, making the remark, "You need not be uneasy about the money, for So-and-so (the bankers) will tell you I am all right, and when you send the things home you shall be paid. I am Joe Smith, from whom some time ago you took a watch he bought from you when he came to your store, and gave him the full value for it when he was in want of money," and so departed, having shown his gratitude by buying 6000*l.* worth of jewellery. This worthy miner is now one of the wealthy pillars of the State.

The Chinese quarter of San Francisco has been described, I will not say *ad nauseam*, but as often as any book has been written which contains an ac-account of a visit to the city of the Golden Gate. Of course we went there, and saw all that was to be seen under the best possible auspices, for Mr. Bee, whom I have already mentioned, was our guide and companion, assisted by an exceedingly intelligent officer of the police force; and on the occasion of our second visit, when we went to the theatre, we had the advantage of being under the protection of the gentleman who represents law and order, on behalf of the municipality, in connection with the Chinese population and the arrangements for theatrical performances.

The inspection of the dreadful den in which the opium-smokers were to be seen suggested to my mind a train of thought in connection with the traffic which I would not willingly have communicated to my American friends. It will seem incredible some day to the awakened conscience of the nation that we should have ever sanctioned such a frightful crime as the opium traffic. "It only poisons about two millions of people," is the excuse, "and brings in one-sixth of the whole revenue of India." If ever it were justifiable to utter the exclamation "Perish India!" it would be, I believe, in regard to that disgraceful source of revenue, and the necessity that is imposed upon us, as it is alleged, to raise it, in order to maintain the government of our Indian empire. Here in San Francisco the State has nothing to do with the sale of the poison, and it is very questionable whether the police regulations should not be applied to it, just as they are to persons who have tried to commit suicide, or to the inebriates in public-houses, or to places where intemperance is carried on to an extent injurious to the public peace. Death is the inevitable result of continued indulgence in opium-smoking, although it is true that in some cases the victim lingers on a few years, utterly indifferent to all the

business of life except the one—the means of supply-
ing himself with his only source of enjoyment. I was
in one of the shops where they sell the drug, and was
much struck by the cadaverous, sunken faces of the
unfortunate customers, with bright dreamy eyes,
trembling limbs, and wasted bodies, who came in to
buy it. It is cheap enough, in all conscience, as a
very small quantity suffices to produce what is called
"the desired effect"; but for its bulk it is exceedingly dear, and indulgence in it must consume a
considerable amount of the earnings of the best-paid
artisans when they are no longer able to earn sufficient
to keep them with a full supply. "Then," as our informant says, "they will commit any crime to get it."

The general impression made upon me by the appearance of the Chinese population was most favourable. I do not now speak of what one might see in
going through the haunts where the police regulations assign exclusive possession to certain classes
of the population, which, sooth to say, seemed numerous enough; I refer to the business quarters, and to
the crowds of cleanly, intelligent, well-behaved people
of both sexes in the streets. General McDowell, and
many other persons, for whose opinion the greatest
respect must be entertained, look with apprehen-
sion on the effect of the Chinese immigration, and
have, indeed, declared that it will destroy the Union
if it be not checked; and these apprehensions are
based upon the possibility that in time millions on
millions of the swarming population of China will

inundate the United States, gradually overrun town
after town, usurping all the fields of labour, and beating down the white man to the greatest misery by
competition in every branch of trade, industry, and
labour. This party has successfully, I believe, impressed its views upon a considerable number of
senators and representatives in the Eastern States,
who can exercise pressure on the Supreme Government; and the treaty recently signed between the
Republic and China contains provisions which enable
the authorities at the western seaports to exercise
considerable control over the current of emigration.
But, on the other hand, it is alleged that the fears
which are expressed of a rapidly increasing exodus of
Chinese from China, and an anabasis into the United
States, are purely imaginary—in fact, unreal and pre-
tentious. The pro-Chinese party allege that the
emigration comes from only one port in one province,
and that you may go all over the West, and ask any
Chinaman or Chinawoman where he or she comes
from, and you are met with the invariable answer,
from the one port. The friends of the Chinese—arguing,
moreover, that the State at large is benefited enormously by the accession to its resources from the Celestial Empire, and that the labour was attacked, not
because it was cheap, but because it was good; that it
is now indispensable, for without Chinamen and China-
women it would be almost impossible to carry on the
ordinary life of these cities—allege that the agitation
which has been so violent in San Francisco is mainly

encouraged by those who want to secure the Irish vote. Colonel Bee represents these views very strongly. He argues that Canton, not larger than the State of New Hampshire, is the sole source of emigration. He insists on it that there are no more than 100,000 Chinese in the whole of the Union, and that for the last ten years the emigrants have not sufficed to fill the places of those who had gone home with money, never intending to return, or who had died. He maintains, indeed, that the Chinese are decreasing rather than otherwise; and with all the power of figures, which he has at his fingers' ends as Consul, demonstrates that a very large proportion of the Chinese who are entered as arriving at San Francisco and other parts are the same men and women as those who came some years previously and went back to their native country, returning to gain more dollars.

The principal enemies of the Chinese are the Irish, who, having monopolised the whole of the work of bricklayers, plasterers, carters, porters, and general labourers until their arrival, have been forced to reduce their rates of labour steadily by the competition of the Chinaman.

The part of the population of San Francisco denominated the Sand lot, and especially those connected with the political associations of the city, do not by any means share Colonel Bee's views; but the agitation is dying out, and the meetings, which were of weekly occurrence, to excite the people against the Mongolians have decreased in number, importance, and interest.

The directors of public companies, and the contractors for public works, are all in favour of the Chinese workman, who is sober, industrious, and orderly; and although the trade combinations among them are exceedingly subtle, and their powers of association for trade purposes remarkable, being moreover the most ancient in the world, the Chinese in the Western States have not as yet taken to indulge in the luxury of strikes. As domestic servants, nurses, and attendants on children, they appear to be affectionate and careful; and nothing could be better than the service of the hotel in which we were lodged, the great portion of which was carried on by Chinamen and women.

June 10th.—In the spacious courtyard of the Palace Hotel, at 7 o'clock this morning, there might have been observed three well-appointed waggons (as Americans call the vehicle more appropriately termed "spider" at the Cape), each with two horses of race, fast trotters, panting for a spin through the city and the Park out to the shores of the Pacific. The Duke and Sir H. Green and Mr. Stephen were driven by Mr. Howard. Mr. Wright was "personally conducted" by Mr. ———, and I was put behind a pair of as handsome chestnuts as could well be seen anywhere, of which the owner and driver (General Barnes) was very reasonably proud. The streets of San Francisco, like those of most of the American cities we have visited, are atrociously paved; the torture of driving over boulders is aggravated by the sharp ribs of the tramways, so that it is not pleasant, if, indeed, it be possible, to drive rapidly till the limit of municipal incompetence or fraud be passed. But once out on the suburbs the chestnuts were invited to step it, and were bowling along at a good fourteen miles an hour on our way to the Park, over as good a road as horse or man ever felt under hoof or foot. The Park not long ago was a waste of sand, it is now swarded and planted with shrubs, and luxuriant with flowers. Notices that it was unlawful to do more than ten miles an hour were posted up, but the General did not pay strict attention to them till he came near shady places, where experience warned him that policemen might be lying privily in ambush. The pace was quickened till the waggon seemed to fly through the air rather than move over the ground. It was the perfection of travelling on wheels—almost as buoyant as a headlong gallop. The waggon weighed but 180 lb., the powerful animals " scarcely felt it more than their tails." I had a turn at the reins by " kind permission " of the General. The art of driving trotters needs practice. You must keep a strong, steady pull on the head, or they " break." Very soon I had the satisfaction of making the chestnuts break the law with a vengeance, and of hearing the General say, " We are just within the three minutes! not ten seconds inside it ! "—that is, of trotting at the rate of just twenty miles an hour. Up hill and down hill, and along the flat out of the Park and over the smooth road, and in half an hour the Pacific was in sight, and the murmurs of the surf rose above the rhythm of the regular beat of the eight hoofs in front of us! Cliff House was in view. Seal Rocks, in their setting of foam, lay before us, and in forty minutes from the time we left the hotel, despite policemen, miles of bad pavements, and tramways, we drew up at the steps of Cliff House, nine miles from San Francisco, and the trotters had not turned a hair. From the verandah at the sea front of the hotel, we enjoyed for half an hour a spectacle which is, as far as I know, unique. At the distance of 500 or 600 yards from the beach at our feet there is a group of four very rugged rocks, with serrated edges and tops, the sides broken here and there into ledges and small platforms. They are too small to be called islands, the largest being, as it seemed, not 100 yards wide. The slopes are not, I think, so steep as they looked on the land side. On the two largest of these rocks there were herds of sea-lions, so close that we could see, through very poor opera-glasses, with the greatest ease, their eyes, teeth, and whiskers, as they reposed or played with each other. Some had clambered to the highest ledges, escalading the sides by a series of painful-looking struggles with their flappers; others were fast asleep in cosy nooks; some were tossing their heads about and making believe to bite each other in sport; the younger ones were bent on teasing their fathers and mothers by uncouth gambols. As they played or moved they uttered cries between a bark and a roar; now and then the noise was like that of a pack of hounds in full cry, and the effect of the strange sound mingling with the tumult of the surf and the beat of the waves was most singular and "eldrich." Those fresh from the sea were shining black, but became lighter as they dried. The older ones were not darker than cinnamon bears or unwashed sheep. As many of those on the rocks had not long left the water the general effect of the herd put one in mind of a gathering of enormous slugs on cabbages—not a poetic simile, but a just one, I think. Occasionally a sea-lion, hungry or bored by his companions, threw himself with a splash into the wave, and it was interesting to watch the rapidity and actual grace of his movements in the sea compared with his laborious efforts on the land. One could see them quite clearly through the body of the heavy billows; occasionally a bold one would glide close on shore and fish in the edge of the surf, raising his head and shoulders clear above the surface, and then diving out of sight. They were cruising about in every direction. You remember the sea-lion at the Zoo, of which the French attendant was so fond? Well, the creatures below and before us were most of them double the size of that fellow, and several exceeded the largest ox in size. The monsters are quite well known; one is named Ben Butler, "because he is such a great beast." They were formerly protected by law, but some one thought they killed too many fish, and the law was repealed. They are safe all the same, for there is a law against the discharge of fire-arms within 300 yards of an inhabited dwelling; Cliff House throws its ægis over the sea-lions in that wise;

u *t* the quantity of fish which must be devoured by these mountainous phocæ (an they be so) daily would maintain a decently-sized city. The hide furnishes the "sealskin" used to cover trunks, and the body yields oil fat, and the tusks are close, white, and hard. These sea-lions breed far away up north, and come with their young regularly every year to the same resorts; but incessant war is waged upon them by the sealers and whalers, so that the chances are against the beast where he is not protected by law, and their numbers do not increase. Altogether, the spectacle was one never to be forgotten. A hotel, with oysters awaiting us for a forebreakfast refection in the background, waggons from Michigan, horses from Kentucky, all the apparatus of civilised life close at hand, the Pacific and its strange wild denizens at our feet! "Let us turn in and have an oyster." "What! oysters in June?" "Yes, and good ones too." In this favoured land oysters are in season all the year round. There are no oysters found on the coast, I am told, and they will not breed. They are brought all the way from the Atlantic coast when they are mere oysterlets, and they are laid down in the Pacific, where they grow fat and large, but are not "crossed in love," and therefore are fit to be eaten from January to January. They are about the size of a spring chicken, and need some courage on the part of an assailant who desires to dispose of them as he would a native.

This was our last day in the city of the Golden Gate, and the photographers were masters of the situation;

and there was much *débris* of sight-seeing to sweep up
—visits to be made, shops to be inspected, among
which I must mention specially the Diamond Palace
of Colonel Andrews, one of the handsomest jeweller's
"stores" in the world, though it is not as large as the
establishments of the principal firms in London, Paris,
Vienna, or as Tiffany's in New York. The distinctive
feature of the interior is the decoration of the paintings
of fair women, on the ceiling and the walls above the
cases, by necklaces, diadems, zones, and other feminine
ornaments of real diamonds, emeralds, rubies, and
pearls. The pictures are the work of an Italian artist
of merit, and the general effect is very striking; but I
doubt whether it is a good way of inducing people to
buy the articles which bedeck the ideal beauties. At
Bradley and Rulofson's we saw photographs of many
of our friends, and had one more proof of the smallness
of the world. Every one we knew seemed to have
visited San Francisco. There we all submitted to
inevitable fate, and left our negatives behind us, but
the Duke was captured by a rival photographic institution, and had a sitting all to himself.

The aspect of a crowd in a large American city
differs from that of the passers-by in the street of an
English town, most of all in the appearance of such
a large proportion of coloured people. Here it may be
said, however, that they are colourless, as the prevail-
ing hue of the foreign population is that of the Chinaman. In Canada the number of negroes, or of persons
of negro descent, of varying gradations of colour, is

remarkable, considering the circumstances, but they
probably may be accounted for by the emigration in
the olden times of those who were escaping from
slavery, or who went with their masters and emplóyers
into the Dominion.   In the cities on the Lakes I was
very much struck by the persons of undoubted African
descent who are to be met with in the streets in great
numbers ; and in Chicago there is a quarter nearly
exclusively occupied by them—honest, industrious,
hard-working people seemingly, given to stand about
at the street corners, however, a good deal on Sundays, and cultivating a bright attire, especially on the
part of the ladies, whose bonnets and shawls were
things to wonder at.   There are loafers amongst them,
as there are amongst their betters ; but, taking them
all in all, in the Northern, Western, and Atlantic
States, they are a decidedly useful element in the
population, easing the burden of labour to the white
man, and following many occupations, such as those of
waiters, barbers, bricklayers, and labourers in the less
skilled sort of work, for which it would be difficult to
find American substitutes.   One peculiarity, which
may be accounted for by some wiser person than
myself, seems to be their recklessness as to what
they put on their heads.   Whether it is merely a
compliance with the custom of the white man, which
impels them to cover the highly effective protection
against sun and cold which Nature has given them, or
not ; or whether it is that the canons of taste in such
matters have not yet settled down to those accepted by

people in civilised life in the Western world, the male
negro has the most extraordinary indifference as to
the quality and shape of the thing which he calls a
hat or cap, and it would not be easy to find out of the
gutters of some Irish country town anything more
dilapidated, battered, and utterly incoherent than
some of the hats which one may see on the heads of
people of colour, especially down South. Whatever
other virtues they may have, neatness is not amongst
them; for, with all their affectation of finery, their
clothes are generally ill-kept, their houses are un-
kempt, and, where they are cultivators of the soil, the
operations are performed in a slovenly manner. The
traditions of the old plantation have descended upon
them, and influence them.

On my way from Messrs. Donahue and Kelly, the
bankers in Montgomery Street—I believe the former
of these gentlemen has had the privilege of giving
his name to steamers and cities, leastways railway
stations—I saw a party of sailors belonging to the
United States steamer "*Rodgers*," now about to proceed in search of the "*Jeannette*," and I was much
struck by their resemblance to our own bluejackets
in general "cut of the jib," dress, face, and figure.
They were in charge of a smart-looking officer, and
had been paying a farewell visit to the fruit and
vegetable markets—one of the sights of the city.
They were in high good-humour, laughing and chat-
ting loudly, more than is the wont of Americans,
and I could not but contrast their fine physique with

that of the soldiers we had seen at Sir Henry Green's parade when General McDowell took us round the harbour. The detachment at the Fort, consisting of infantry and artillerymen, and squads of different regiments, had some weedy veterans in the ranks, who had lost their setting up and did not look fit for much work; but the sailors, probably a picked lot, were good all round.

À *propos* of Messrs. Donahue and Kelly, the number of wealthy men in San Francisco of Irish origin or nationality is remarkable. Millionaires with names of Milesian prefixes and terminations are phenomenal. We had intended to return to the East Coast by way of Utah, and to stay a day or two at Salt Lake City, but the railroad company did not consider it expedient to give the party the facilities which had been accorded in every other instance by the American authorities to the Duke and his friends. To have gone round Salt Lake City would have cost a couple of hundred pounds more for haulage, and we were much more interested in seeing Leadville and Denver than the City of the Mormons; the game was not thought to be worth the candle, and it was resolved that we would go back as we came, in charge of the representatives of the Atchison, Topeka, and Santa Fé Railroad Company. It was only one item more in the long list of things we ought to have seen if we could, and I can safely say that we had a large share of the common experience of travellers in regard to the relations between the possible and the impossible in the course of a journey in a strange land, where there are for ever cropping up representations that "you really ought not to leave without seeing" so and so. The evening of our last day was passed in the society of General McDowell, Mr. Morgan, the English Consul, Colonel Bee, and others, who had done so much to make the visit to San Francisco all that could be desired, and whose courtesy and kindness will ever be remembered by every one of us most gratefully. Like Sir Charles Coldstream, we "had seen everything, done everything," but, unlike him, had found there was plenty in it. The street railway—most ingenious and successful, invaluable in a hilly city like Lisbon—the Chinese Theatre, the Joss houses—shops, eating-houses, opium dens of the Chinese quarter, the clubs, the principal buildings, the streets, the shops, the markets, the harbour, the suburbs, and country round about—all had been inspected, and yet each day we were told that we were doing positive injustice to ourselves and to the objects which were perforce neglected. In the morning there was a levée in the hotel to bid the Duke good-bye and see the party start on their return journey. At the very last moment a gentleman came forward with a proposal to take us to the North Pole by balloon, but there was not time to consider it in all its bearings and the offer was declined with thanks. We started at 10 A.M., and the Duke was attended to the boat and to the station across the water by a large body of San Franciscans, who took leave ere the train started.

The gentlemen who were with us on the journey
westwards attended the Duke on his way towards
the Eastern States. All day we travelled through
California—" the hot furnace "—which at first, however, proved to be only very warm, and the coloured
servants had constant supplies of iced compounds to
be drunk for the solace of the homeward bound, and
had laid in a stock of San Franciscan luxuries to
soothe the way.

CHAPTER IV.

CALIFORNIA TO COLORADO.

Los Angeles—Mud-geysers—"Billy the Kid"—General Fremont
—Manitou, the Garden of the Gods—Desperadoes—Bob Ingersoll
—Denver City—Leadville—Grand Cañon.

June 12th.—The train stopped at Los Angeles at six
in the morning, and, drawing up my window-blind, the
first person I saw on the platform was our good friend
Colonel Baker, who had come to meet us, intent on the
good offices which he could render during our stay.
These were exhibited in the form of a beautiful bouquet
for Lady Green, baskets of limes and oranges, and
great bunches of grapes. In this happy valley there
are cares as in the rest of the world. The Colonel
told us he was in the midst of a great litigation
affecting his claim to a large tract of land in which
there are said to exist the richest tin-mines in the
American Continent. Yet why should he care about
his tin-mine? There were rolling acres rich with
corn and fruit, and there were flocks and herds and
vineyards, and a charming home of his own. Nevertheless, if the want of that tin-mine made him at all
unhappy, I am sure those who were indebted to him,
as we were, for so many kindnesses, will wish his claim

to be triumphantly asserted, and long possession of all that is to follow.

I dreaded the passage of the Desert to Yuma; and indeed the heat was intense. No wonder that with the thermometer ranging from 100° to 104°, all the blinds in the car were pulled down, and we sprawled listlessly on the cushions. Our excellent attendants put forth all the resources of art in the shape of ice and preparations of limes and cocktails; but the temperature would not be baffled. We could just read, and were aware that we were living, and some of us had strength enough now and then to execute forays against flies with napkins to drive them out of the carriages. How could people live out in the open, and work in the mines, or pursue any out-of-door employment in such torrid heat? Nevertheless, there was a marked distinction between it and the heat to be endured with the mercury at an equal height in India.

The speed of the train was very respectable—somewhat over twenty miles an hour—and at that rate we ran from San Gorgonio and Banning on to Cabazon, through a flat plain, dry and burnt up, very like the desert around Suez, and fringed, like it, with rocky and rugged hills, save that there was a great growth of Spanish bayonets and cactuses of all kinds among the stones and sand, and that snow was to be seen on all the hill-tops in the distance. For 107 miles there was no water to be met with going along this plain; but the mirage, of which I have spoken in the account of our journey to San Francisco, was frequent and beautiful; and again I was fascinated by the sight of lovely lakes embowered in trees, with stately cities on their shores, changing and shifting and melting away, only again to assume apparent substance to cheat the senses.

Once the train stopped to allow the passengers to visit the mud-geysers, which were not more than 150 yards on the left of the line, and with commendable curiosity most of us got out and walked over the baked earth to the spot. There was no mark whatever of smoke or vapour to indicate the place; and it was almost startling to come suddenly upon a kind of pond of semi-liquid mud, fifty or sixty feet in diameter, on which huge bubbles, varying in size from an orange to a hogshead, were continually forming and bursting. There was a faint sulphurous smell, and the ground around the liquefied portion of the surface, where the bubbles were breaking, was hot and cracked. The conductor said that all attempts to reach the bottom of the holes through which the bubbles arose had failed. Two of these geysers were in active operation, and the plain away to the left of the rail was said to contain a great number of them. After all it was very unsatisfactory to see this ebullition going on without being able to account for it; and, generally, I think we thought less of each other and of our information after visiting them, and finding out that not one of us had any theory on the subject which would bear either fire or water.

I do not think I ever saw a sunset more beautiful

than that which marked the close of this day—
certainly not in India or South Africa, nor on the
prairie, for which they make claims of surpassing
beauty in the matter of sunsets. As it died out, I
felt that "thing of beauty" could not "be a joy for
ever," for it was a combination of colour and of form,
including sky and mountain, that it would be impossible to see again.

The kindness of which we have had so many
proofs, has followed, accompanied, and preceded us
all unremittingly and unweariedly. A rough with
some Bourbon on board mounted to-day the steps
of the car at a station, and insisted on seeing "this
Duke." When he was told that the object of his
attention was engaged, he said, "This is a land of
liberty (as in his case it was), and he doesn't want a
bodyguard with him!" But the conductor sent him
away about his business without trouble. On the
platform at Benson a few miners asked "the Duke to
come out and show himself." The people at the stations
were generally satisfied with a quiet peep; now and
then an enthusiastic Scotchman claimed a shake hands,
which was always accorded to him. A sleeper placed
across the rails (accounted for by the officers on the
hypothesis that some loafer without a ticket had been
turned off by the conductor, and had put the sleeper in
the way of the train to wreak his vengeance—a thing
which has occurred nearer home) was the only substantial danger to which we were here exposed.

The heat (June 13th) was intense. The thermometer

rose to 105 at one o'clock in the day, and it was little comfort to us to be told that at Deming it had been up to 110 the day before.

For some days we have been supping full of horrors, indeed breakfasting and dining on them, for the papers contain accounts of.the extraordinary homicides all about this region. Tucson, Benson, Wilcox—all these places were resounding with the exploits of " Billy the Kid." Now at Tucson there is, I believe, a man whose name was once amongst the very foremost in the United States. Who some twenty years and more ago had not heard of General Fremont, " the Pathfinder," the adventurous traveller, the energetic politician, the dashing soldier ? He had gone at the outbreak of the war to take up the chief command in the west with all the pomp and circumstance of glorious war. I was somewhat astonished to find that he was at Tucson, the governor of the Territory, on a humble salary, apparently the world-forgetting and the world-forgot, while " Billy-the-Kid " was perpetrating numberless atrocities under his nose, and Mr. Pat Garrett was dressing up his loins with his revolver-belt, and about to go forth with a chosen band of citizens and seek the redoubtable William.*

A person who has only seen settled States in Europe, or the Eastern States of the North American Continent, cannot form any notion of a territory

* IIow Mr. Garrett executed his mission and killed the Kid is narrated in the account of the desperados of the West, which forms a separate chapter.

which has become a centre of attraction to all the wild adventurers and daring spirits which society, in the process of formation, throws out as a sort of advanced guard. In Arizona, in 1870, according to the American Almanac, out of a total population of 9658, 2729 could not write and 2690 could not read. Of the total population 2491 were foreign born, and 2753 were natives, the rest being coloured or under ten years of age. In New Mexico, out of 91,000 people, 48,000 over ten years of age could not read, and 51,000 whites over ten years of age could not write. It may be inferred from such figures what is the general condition of the labouring classes in these States and Territories. The inhabitants of these States have doubled in the last ten years. They are filling up at a rate inconceivably great—so great, indeed, that American newspapers are fairly bewildered and American statesmen appalled by the rush across the Rocky Mountains and down the rivers, although as yet but a small proportion of the immense stream of immigrants has flooded the outlying territories. "At this rate," exclaims a Western editor, "the old monarchies of Europe will soon be depopulated." When Mr. Lincoln, in 1861, addressed his inaugural to the expectant States he expressed his confident belief that there were children then born who would live to see the flag of the Union floating over no less than 100,000,000 of human beings. The recent census of the United States gives a return of 51,000,000 of people, but the most eminent statisticians have arrived at the belief that the progress

and increase of the States will not be at the same
rapid rate as that which marked the history of the
Republic since the cessation of the great civil war.
It may be fairly inferred, however, that at the end
of this century the population of the United States
will greatly exceed that of Russia, or that of any
empire except China and Great Britain, including
Hindostan. The population, on each period of ten
years, has increased at an average of more than 30
per cent. ; in fact, nearer 33 per cent., and the centre
of it has travelled westward at the rate of more than
fifty miles every ten years, till the centre of population is now eight miles west by south from Cincinnati.
In 1800 the Union extended over only 239,935 square
miles. Its flag now floats over 1,272,239 square miles
of States and over 1,800,000 square miles of Territory
governed by the central power at Washington. " We
cannot think," exclaims a Republican writer, " that
the war of rebellion settled all our troubles and made
us secure in our Republic. This enormous growth
of the practically unknown West reveals to us the
grave dangers that threaten our nation. We meet
there the tremendous influences of alien races and alien
religions." The Americans of New England and of the
Eastern States do not feel anxious on that score,
because their institutions are thoroughly founded,
their character formed, and they trust to the great
power of accomplished facts to assimilate the alien
elements and sustain the fabric of the Republic. The
bugbear of a great Chinese immigration has ceased to

practically influence Californian politics, and it may be safely assumed that the bulk of the future immigrants from the Celestial Empire will only come from the same sources as those which have hitherto supplied the stream. No wonder, however, that thoughtful Americans—and there are many who think of the future of their country as something quite apart from dollars—are filled with grave anxieties when they see such floods of purely foreign material, which will in all probability exercise a preponderating influence over the politics of the Great Republic, surging into the States. Particularly have the home missionary clergy, as they are styled, been struck by the enormous influence which this foreign immigration has exercised. According to one authority, the Rev. Mr. Stimson, of Worcester, "it is not a question of spreading any particular form of Christianity or of Church government, but a momentous struggle of American institutions with alien civilisations and religions for the control of the great Western country. The problem is not a matter of cleaning door-yards, but of saving a continent for freedom." The Chinese Question and the Indian Question are, they think, as nothing compared with the Irish Question and the German Question. "The Republic," we are told, "stands on a foundation as broad as humanity itself," whatever that may mean, "but its condition of existence is a universal regard for the interests of all." Often during the course of the Duke of Sutherland's excursion it was our good fortune to fall in with men of great political and social knowledge. The future of the Republic is, in the mind of these men, clouded with uncertainty and doubt. They are apprehensive of some unknown danger. It may be corruption of political life leading to want of faith in free institutions; it may be the rival energies and the opposing interests which Washington foresaw as likely to array the East against the West—the Atlantic States against the inland States, and it is calculated by some sanguine people that before this century is over there will be eighteen, or possibly twenty, States admitted into the Union formed out of the Territories which are now under the central Government at Washington. Upon such influences as these alien immigration may be expected to act with prodigious power. At a recent meeting in Springfield a clergyman gave as an illustration of the absolute indifference of the foreign immigrants to Republican institutions a conversation he had with a Norwegian minister in Minneapolis. "There is nothing," said this gentleman, "in America which we Norwegians regard as of value except your land and your money. We do not want to learn English: we do not want to know the Americans around us; we have certainly no notion of becoming Americans, but we intend to remain as we are—Norwegians." The Mormons control Utah. They boast that they will soon govern five of the most important territorial regions beyond the Rockies. But if Utah becomes a State, as she hopes to do, she will found a Mormon code of laws and institutions beyond the power of the United States to control. New Mexico may be considered as a Roman Catholic State under the control of an excellent archbishop. Of course all prophecies may be falsified by events, but judging by the eighty years which have elapsed of the present century, and from the ratio of increase in that time in the United States, the most liberal construction may be placed even upon the bounding estimates of American politicians and statists. When we look to the Far West and see, for instance, how Winnipeg has become the centre of a great network of river navigation, 300 miles in one direction, 600 miles in another, and that the Mackenzie River passes for 1200 miles through what is declared to be the future wheat region of the world, we may easily comprehend the anxiety with which the patriotic American is filled lest the future of such a State should fall into hands antagonistic to the principles in which his *beau idéal* of government has been founded and has prospered.

June 14.—At Lamy, a station named after the good archbishop of Santa Fé, where we halted for a short time whilst the passengers of another train were breakfasting, a citizen came up to me on the platform and exclaimed, as if he were very much impressed by the news he was going to give, "If you look in there, sir, you will see Bob Ingersoll at breakfast!" I asked whether there was anything very remarkable about the fact. "Well, sir," he said, "he is Colonel Ingersoll, of whom you have heard. He is the most remarkable in-fidel in the United States, and I really think he believes what he preaches. A good man to look at, too, and, they say, first-rate in his family." I had a glance at the believer in unbelief, and saw a very presentable-looking person, of fine appearance and good features, busily engaged in making the most of his time at one of the tables in the refreshment-room. He was the observed of all observers, and appeared to like it; and I understood from one of the crowd that he had just returned from inspecting some mining ventures in which he was concerned; for, if he does not believe in the world to come, he is credited with very strong faith in the excellencies of the possession of wealth in the world that is. His lectures are attended by crowded audiences, but, as an astute American observed, "they won't come to much, for, after all, people who do not believe anything can never get up a great enthusiasm. It is in believing something that the populace has faith."

Once more our eyes were rejoiced with the sight of the lovely plains of Las Vegas, wide-spreading fields decked with flowers and dotted with flocks, bordered with ranges of softly contoured mountains, the courses of the water streams indicated by bright vegetation and by growth of trees of many kinds. From Lamy (170 miles) there is a gradual rise to Raton, which we reached at 6.30 in the evening. The appearance of the region we traverse as the train approaches the Raton Pass presents a strong contrast to the desolate country through which we have been passing. From Raton the train was drawn by two engines in front and shoved by one behind, and even then the pace was not very rapid, for the ascent is very sharp. All the more could we enjoy a very glorious sunset, as we slowly ascended the mountain. Then darkness came on rapidly, and we slid down towards La Junta into the night, and were all fast asleep long before we arrived there. In the very early morning, on June 15th, some two hours after midnight, we halted for a time at Pueblo. At 9 o'clock we had to leave our beloved Pullman and change the cars, for we were to take a fresh point of departure, starting from the Union Depôt upon the Denver and Rio Grande narrow-gauge railway for Denver, 119 miles distant, and making an excursion on the way to Manitou, to which we diverged from Colorado Springs : for to go within reach of that famous resort and not to see it would have been a great outrage on all the rules and regulations established for the observance of travellers. Certes narrow-gauge railways need an apology. Their *raison d'être* is, at the best, that they are better than nothing. "If you won't have us, you can have nothing else." And in such a mountainous region as we were about to visit, the difficulties and expense connected with a broad-gauge line would have been enormous, if indeed it could be constructed at all. The narrow-gauge carriages, with seats to match, with which we were made acquainted for the first time, were of course much less commodious and comfortable than those we had quitted, but far superior to those on the Indian lines of the same gauge, and Indian engineers had been over to take a lesson from the Americans for the use of their carriage-builders. Atchison, Topeka, and Santa

Fé Company and Denver and Rio Grande Company have been at daggers drawn and pistols cocked—ay, and fired—and at battles waged, in times gone by; and now our friends on the former line were, like ourselves, the guests of the latter, which was represented by several official gentlemen anxious to do the honours to the Duke. The scenery becomes grander and wilder every mile as the special hurries on as well as it can over the sinuous line, which is piercing a mountain region savage and sterile, and climbing by the sides of ravines and creeping upwards in rocky valleys with pine-clad hill-tops and frowning cliffs above. The engineer who designed the line is a Scotchman named McMurtrie —or at least of recent Scotch origin—and he seems to have a special gift for such aspiring work, and a gradient-compelling genius not to be baffled by altitudes. We were mounting towards the snows. Range upon range of whitened summits and hoary ridges came in view, all paying homage to the rugged crown of Pike's Peak, which can be seen from points more than 140 miles away. The fleecy cloudland which seemed to lie before us, as we looked away from Pueblo, was resolving itself into savage alps. And in these passes, which the eye caught for a moment, there might be El Dorados still undiscovered, for around us were cities springing out of the desert. Here the enchanter's wand is the explorer's pick, and no one could say where the precious ore might not be awaiting its touch. We were coming to the Land of Promises. The conversation of our new friends, among whom were some gentlemen of the press, related mostly to mines, and one of them had, as we discovered, a very certain investment at the disposal of the Duke, in the form of a mining-claim, which was worth, at the lowest computation, twice as much as he was willing to take for it. There was no reason to doubt his good faith, but it was felt that it was a kind of fortune which ought not to pass into the hands of strangers, and should be reserved for the people of the country ; and I am sure all of the party who had the pleasure of the owner's acquaintance hope that he has "made his pile" out of it, and has more than realised his expectations.

Colorado Springs, forty-five miles from Pueblo, is nearly 6000 feet above the level of the sea. The character of the line to it is best described in the fact that the average grade per mile is 44·14, the maximum curvature 6°. There are "no Springs" here, but the little town, charmingly situated, is a halting-place much frequented in tourist-time by travellers, and reputed to be healthful. There are some pleasant houses visible from the station, at which we descended to take our places in the carriages provided to take us to Manitou Springs, five miles away. Mr. Palmer—if General, I beg his pardon—the President of the Railroad, had important business to attend to, but he was so well represented by Mr. Bell, the Vice-President, that no one regretted his absence, and it cannot be said in his case *les absents ont toujours tort.* He is reported to have made a very large fortune with much ingenuity, and to have business talents which even in this country excite admiration. Mr. Bell is an Irish gentleman, a member of the medical profession, who has a delightful villa embowered in a garden in the environs of Manitou, where the Duke and his friends found a charming interior and an Irish-American welcome, and discovered that strawberries and cream were almost as good in Colorado as in Covent Garden. A quaint, odd place, Manitou—an American Martigny, with Pike's Peak rising (14,300 feet above the sea) over it in the clear sky, inspiring regret that we could not make the excursion to the summit, which is rewarded, we were told, and I can believe, by one of the grandest views in the world—the usual service of guides, horses, and mules, and *caleches*—a naturalist's store with skins, minerals, feathers, and stuffed " objects " — detached wooden houses and villas in small plots of garden—a straggling street, and large hotels for invalids. But there was the unusual feature of encampments here and there by the roadside, and notices forbidding the pitching of tents within certain limits which were explained by the fact that the high reputation of the waters and air induces people to come from great distances for the treatment of consumption, and diseases of throat and lungs. Many of them find it cheaper to travel in horse waggons and pitch their canvas dwellings when they wish to make a halt, than to take up their quarters at hotels. Poor people! what pale, hectic cheeks and wasted forms we saw; little groups picnicking by the sides of the rivulets along the roads—each with a gnawing care-anxiety about some dear one's health in the midst of them. Our driver, an intelligent, chatty lad, was full of information, and we had to drive the prescribed road by the wells out to the Ute Pass, a mountain-gorge wild enough—a small *Tête Noire*—to points to which magniloquent names have been given.

It is not for want of what is called puffing that Americans neglect the resorts of health of their own country, and in the States far and wide the beauties and advantages of Manitou are blazoned forth on the walls of hotels and in guide-books to all who can read. I may confess now that, notwithstanding the magnificent altitude of Pike's Peak, and the eccentric forms of the rocks in the "Garden of the Gods," I was disappointed with Manitou. But then the visit was short, and the day was hot, and the way was long and dusty, and haply it might be that under different circumstances Manitou would deserve much warmer praise. It possesses indeed an abundance of curious springs, said to be full of health-giving properties; and in the course of our drive we halted several times to partake of drinks from various springs, out of one one of which bubbled up very good soda-water, precisely like Schweppe's best in taste and appearance. At the large hotel, which put one in mind of the great establishments of the same sort in Switzerland, the water served at table to the guests—a sort of pleasant Apollinaris-tasting beverage—came from a natural fountain.

The "cataract" nearly made us angry, and there was no regret felt when the carriages returned to the hotel, where there was unwonted activity and bustle, as the "Denver Zouaves" had just descended in a friendly razzia on it, and were desolating the hearts and fireside resources of Manitou. The consequences might have been serious, as it turned out, to unoffending strangers. Those who needed it turned into the barber's shop of the hotel to be shaved, and after some delay a coloured man appeared, who began to try his hand on me. Fortunately it was not 'prentice, for it was very unsteady, and I became a little alarmed for my cuticle. "It will be all right, mister," quoth the barber. "I never cut any one. But I'm demoralised, dat's a fact, having to wait on dem Denver Zouaves. Lor a messy on any enemy dey has! My nerve's all gone to pieces wid their wantin' everting at once at the dinner!" The hotel seemed far more clean and comfortable than the caravanserais in the land of William Tell; but our stay was short, for we were put under orders for a sight which has the most inappropriate name that could be invented—a valley in which the most extraordinary-looking columns carved out in a plateau by the agency of water, have been left standing, detached and in groups, to which the visitor enters through a cleft in a barrier of rock passing round the base of a pillar of sandstone as high as a house. The "Garden of the Gods" contains 500 acres, and is surrounded by mountains and cliffs. The sandstone pillars generally taper from the base upwards to a short distance from the tops, which are flattened out or surmounted by slabs or blocks of sand-

stone of fantastic outline, and they are called by names
derived from fancied likenesses to animals, birds,
and men. The juxtaposition of the most brilliantly
hued, dazzling-red blocks and strata, with masses of
the same material of milky whiteness, gives the impression that the scene is the work of human hands;
it seems too quaint and artificial for the hand of
Nature, to which alone it is due; and the vegetation
and the trees are in keeping with the character of the
place. A trysting-place for geologists, and their happy
hunting-ground, no doubt. But why "the Garden of
the Gods," I pray?

From the valley or cup, emerging by another
road, the driver took us to a ravine-like recess,
almost girt in by high wooded mountains, in which
Mr. (General?) Palmer is erecting a mansion of pala-
tial importance—a picturesque site surely—cliffs,
forests, and mountain all around, and in view one most
singular sandstone pillar, named the Major Domo,
120 feet high and only 30 feet round—a mountain
stream brawling through tangled brushwood glades
—a garden. But the heat! That must prove a terror
by day to the inmates of Glen Eyrie Lodge or Castle
—which, by the by, was named, as one of us insisted,
from a collection of rubbish on a ledge in the face of
one of the cliffs, which was, he maintained, the nest of
an eagle. It was now time to return to our train,
and we were not sorry to get back to Colorado Springs.

From Colorado Springs to our destination at Denver
there were still 75 miles of rail, and the line con-

tinued to ascend till we reached Divide (7186 feet),
whence there was a gentle descent. There were sixteen stations named on the time-table. We stopped
at very few of them, and travelled somewhat too fast
to permit our placid enjoyment of the scenery, austere
and vast, which indeed deserved more attention than
could be given to it by passengers in a very lively
train—endless alps on alps, not sheeted with perpetual
white, but rather flecked with snowfields, which con-
trasted finely with the sombre pine-forests, and the
rich hues of the rocks, touched by the rays of the
setting sun, that, ere it slid behind the mountains,
cast a rose-coloured mantle on their summit. The
evidences of a bustling city were not wanting in the
approaches to the capital of Colorado. There were
tall chimneys vomiting out smoke in the distance, and
near at hand trains of waggons were toiling over the
dusty plain—still 5000 feet above the sea-level—fast
trotters and people on horseback, beer-gardens, factories of all kinds, brick-kilns, and then a fringe of
log houses and wooden shanties, before the train
stopped at the imposing and substantial depot.

It was a quarter-past eight, nearly dark, when
we reached Denver, and glad were we to get into
the hall of the Windsor Hotel, which was crowded
with a mixed multitude—miners, and speculators, and
traders, and some travellers like ourselves—a very busy
scene indeed. In the hotel were all human comforts
nearly ; hot and cold baths, and good rooms, and more
appliances of civilised existence, for those who could

pay for them, than could be found in many hostelries
of approved reputation in venerable towns at home;
moreover, exuberant offers of help and information.
One goes to bed laden with obligations and heavy with
the sense of favours which can never be repaid. There
was now a *soupçon* of frost in the air, and notwithstanding the heat which we had endured the greater
part of the day, fires were not ungrateful; and as
we peered out of our windows over the roofs of the
wide-spread houses of the town, we could see the
snow on the lofty ranges of hills, watered by the South
Platte River and Cherry Creek, which surround the
cup in which Denver has been built in obedience to
the impulses of the increasing population, which now
numbers, I believe, 38,000 souls. There was a bright
glare from the gas-lighted streets, sounds of music, and
a tumult of life in the town which would have been
creditable to an ancient metropolis. In the morning
from the hotel windows appeared a beautiful and wide-
spread panorama of the hills we had seen the evening
before, peak above peak, none very densely covered
perhaps, or presenting continuous snowfields, but
extending in billowy sweeps far away to the horizon,
all capped with snow, now bathed in a flood of fer-
vent sunshine, the snow lighted up by the peculiar
crimson tints common in Alpine regions. There
were duties in the way of sight-seeing and exploration
of no ordinary nature to be done. First there were
interviews and receptions, and the inevitable drive
through the place as soon as the ordeal of breakfast

was over; and ordeal in some sort it was for the
strangers to file in to the public room and take their
places at their table, aware that the morning papers
had subjected them to exhaustive criticism, which was
being verified by those around us. The morning papers
too had given some topics for reflection, indications
that in the newly created capital of Colorado desperate
men, overtaken by the march of law and order, had
refused to accept service, and were vindicating their
rights as wild western outcasts to take or part with
life as of yore, in reckless encounters and deliberate
assassinations. There were, perhaps, at that moment
some hundreds, if not thousands, out of the population
of 37,000 or 38,000 of the city, who belonged to the
adventurous classes—sporting-men, betting-men, ring-
men, bar-keepers, hell-proprietors, and their satellites,
and the scum of the saloons attracted from the great
cities of the States for hundreds of miles, by the
prey which miners with belts full of gold, half mad
with drink, and always fond of excitement, frequently
are; and if to these be added the dissolute loafers
and broken-down mining speculators, the strength
of the army arrayed against the law may be estimated;
and the wonder is that among a · population armed
to the teeth there are not more cases of such violent
deeds as we were reading of at breakfast. To the
stranger there was no evidence of the existence of
these disturbing elements, unless the bearded and
booted men with speculation in their eyes, in the hotel
passages and halls, belonged to the dangerous, as they

certainly did to the mining, classes. As to the resources of the city, although for rapidity of growth
its wonders may be eclipsed by those of Leadville,
Denver claims a very high place in the catalogue
of these marvellous fungi of civilisation, of which
the Western States present almost unique examples.
There is everything that any one can want to be had
for money in the place, and much more than most people
need. Paris fashions and millinery are in vogue.
There are fine shops, handsome churches, a theatre,
breweries, factories, banks, insurance offices.

The principal street exhibits pretty young people,
who would have no occasion to fear comparison with
the *beau monde* in Eastern or European capitals. The
thoroughfares are crowded with vehicles, and spruce
carriages and well turned-out horses may be seen in
the favourite drive, that has been made over an
indifferent road to the base of the Rocky Mountains,
which appear to be close at hand, though they are
thirteen miles away. But here and there in the well-
dressed crowd may be seen a Bohemian *pur sang*, or a
miner in his every day clothes, bent on a rig out and
a good time of it. The streets, unpaved, dusty, and
rugged, are very wide, and bordered with trees, and
the houses generally are built of good red brick
instead of wood; and there are runnels of water like
those one sees in Pretoria and other Dutch towns in
South Africa. The roads about the city leave much
to be desired; but Rome was not built in a day.

There are many ready-made clothing establishments

in the main streets, and there is a heavy trade in
tinned provisions. Through the Western States, as in
South Africa, the débris of provision-tins constitutes
a certain and considerable addition to the objects to be
seen in the vicinity of every house, and to the mounds
of rubbish in the street of every village. How indeed
could the first-comers in such regions keep body and
soul together without the supplies in such a portable
form of the first necessaries of life? Having once run
up a town in these remote wastes, the inhabitants are
still compelled to make a liberal use of the same sort
of food, and mines of tinned iron gradually accumulate
around them.

Our first excursion was to the Argo Works, under
very pleasant auspices, for we had the wife of the Senator,
who is one of the principal partners, and Mrs. Pearce,
whose husband is largely interested in the works, taking
charge of us. The works are at some distance outside
the town, but the lofty chimneys vomit out quite sufficient vaporous fumes and smoke to blight the vegetation
and to give the people near at hand a taste of their
quality. I am not going to give a minute description,
for more reasons than one, of what we saw at the
works; but it was a very interesting exhibition of the
processes by which the precious metals are extracted
from the ores and delivered to commerce. The Argo
Works simply assay and reduce ores on commission,
but the business is on a very large scale. Immense
piles, in fact small mountains, of brown, cinnamon and
earth coloured dust and rock were heaped up in the

sheds, to be brought to the furnaces and turned, when divested of the lead, iron, copper, and gold, out in ingots of silver. All the methods for the extraction of silver were shown to us, but I committed a gross indiscretion when I asked, in my ignorance, " How do you extract the gold ? " " That," said the urbane gentleman who was conducting us over the works, " we never permit strangers to see." So there is more there than meets the eye.

The business of assaying here must be profitable, and if the reputation of any firm be once established there is a secure fortune for its members. The miners flock to them, and they can dictate terms. The extent of mining work in the country around may be inferred from the numerous offices in connection with it in the city. As a specimen of what Messrs. Bush and Tabor of our hotel give their guests for dinner, let me offer you this *menu* of the 5.30 ordinary to-day (June 16). Soup, beef à l'Anglaise; fish, boiled trout, anchovy sauce ; corned beef, leg of mutton, sirloin beef, chickens with giblet sauce, fricassee à la Toulouse, veal, kidneys sautés aux croûtons, rice, croquettes, baked pork and beans, saddle of antelope, currant jelly, lamb, tongue, chicken salad, spiced salmon ; innumerable " relishes " and vegetables, baked rice pudding, strawberry pie, apricot pie, jelly, blancmange, vanilla, ice cream, macaroons, pound cake, fruit, Swiss cheese, nuts, coffee, &c. The wines were not cheap : champagne 16s. a bottle, St. Julien 6s., Leoville 14s., sherry 8s., brandy 14s. per bottle. Orders for " drinks " at the bar after dinner were much more general than orders for wine at dinner.

Denver, in spite of its mineral wealth, is very poor, however, in that of which the want would make life, even in America, intolerable. The supply of drinking-water is scanty and bad, and last year there was nearly a water famine. The *cartes* in the hotel announced "Water used in this room is boiled and filtered." But great efforts have been made to furnish the inhabitants with a store, constant and adequate, of the precious fluid, and we saw very considerable works, the property of an Irish gentleman, erected before the town attained its present dimensions, which were to be supplemented by a new enterprise respecting which we heard much. Perhaps no town of equal size in an equal length of time has ever had so much money and money's worth flowing in and through it as Denver since the Colorado mines were worked. It is asserted that the trade of the town for 1881 will exceed 8,000,000*l*. Colorado in 1879 yielded ores to the value of more than 3,750,000*l*. The output in the present year will exceed that of 1880. In that year $35,417,517 worth of gold and $20,183,889 of silver (more than 11,000,000*l*.) was deposited in the United States Mint and Assay Office. There is, besides, vast wealth in flocks and herds, and Denver is the place where the people resort from Colorado for purposes of trade and pleasure; altogether an astounding place, with a future quite dazzling to think of, unless the mines give in, and even then Colorado cannot again be poor; its climate and

scenery will always attract travellers, and its capacity
for feeding sheep and cattle will secure its population.
"And as to the beetle?" Why, no·one would have
anything to say to it. Nothing was known of it.
There might be such things in other States. "And
the name?" Probably it was a red-coloured bug, and
got the name Colorado just as the river, or tobacco,
was called, from the hue of it. At all events the bug
did not belong to the State.

The interest which the progress of Colorado and the
condition of society in the State excite was exemplified
by the appearance in Denver of a party of Hungarian
noblemen, whose names gave occasion for stumbling to
the journalists who copied them out of the Hotel Regis-
ter—Count Andrassy and others, who were travelling
under the guidance of Dr. Rudolf Meyer, of Vienna.
Although the air of Denver is so much bepraised,
it happens that most of our party felt rather over-
come at the end of our excursion through the town
and the visit to the smelting works, and one of
the Hungarians was confined to his room. However, they sallied out before dinner, and a gloomy
prophet of evil remarked, "If these strangers should
have a difficulty, I consider they'll hev only their-
selves to blame. Some citizens don't like strangers
comin' in and starin' at them, and they're apt to be
awkward in their tempers in the afternoon." Knowing
no danger, and fearing none, they went off, and were a
long time absent. Meantime we were preparing for
the road, as we were bound for Leadville, the city of

the "biggest boom" of mining times—"the Silver El Dorado," as the guide-book, with a magnificent "bull," describes it. Our Hungarian friends returned to the hotel ere we left. They were filled with enthusiasm, and with a good deal also of curiosity in regard to the shootings of which they had heard so much, and were following in our track next day, and so we parted *sans adieux.* How the love of gold has filled these lone valleys with desperate men! "They are a rough lot, sure enough," said the landlord, "but lynching keeps them down; and it is much better than hanging according to law, to my mind. It certainly is cheaper." "How is it cheaper?" "Why," said he, "when a man is prosecuted, or when he is tried before the judges, the law expenses are heavy, and they fall on the county. When a man is lynched there is only the expense of the rope, and a little loss of time for the boys who do the job." From Denver to Pueblo and from Pueblo to Leadville the line is on the narrow-gauge principle, and our train, which left at seven o'clock in the evening, seemed to be driven on no principle at all; for, anxious to astonish a Duke perhaps, or Britishers generally, the driver did what certainly could not be called his level best to send us along up and down a very rough line, and round the sharpest curves, at the rate of forty miles an hour, so that when we turned in, our rest, if rest at all it were, was exceedingly broken, and we trundled about in our berths as if we were in a ship in a pretty heavy sea. Still this narrow-gauge was the only line which

could be made through such a country as we were
traversing. Peeps out of the window ever and anon
revealed, high up amongst the stars, rugged mountain-
tops, and for ever there came the sound of rushing
water, near or remote, as the train " bounded " on its
course. I do not know what stations we passed on
our way, but the night was very long, and I greeted
with pleasure the first gleam of light above the hill-
tops. The Arkansas River was on our left, and at
dawn we had glimpses of its turbid stream running
madly in deep gorges far below us. At the South
Arkansas station the train halted soon after daybreak,
and then we diverged from the main line, and a light
train took us over the Arkansas River by a fine bridge
on its way up the Gunnison Extension to visit the
highest mountain-pass traversed by a railway in the
world. South Arkansas station is 217 miles from
Denver, and is 6944 feet—and Marshall Pass (25 miles
away), to which we were bound, is 10,760 feet—above
sea-level. There were grades of 211 and curves of 24°
on the way, and the railroad twisted in and out among
the ravines like an iron Alexandrine, for ever ascending
till we had passed the limits of forest life. There were
stations at short intervals—Poncha Springs, Mears,
Silver Creek—from each other. From the stations
there is a good deal of cross-country traffic, and at one
place we saw three stages laden with men and women
—or rather, to be polite and accurate, let me say with
women and ladies—starting, one with six horses, and
the other two with four each. These were bound for

Gunnison, and as we were halting for a little, the Duke and some others got out of the train, and sauntered up towards the wooden shanties which formed " the town," consisting of the usual array of saloons and drinking places. However, our course was cut short by the information vouchsafed by one of the officials, that it might be as well not to go up, as there had been a big shooting match that morning, and that one man was killed and four had been wounded, " and some of them were on the drink yet." From 4.30 A.M. to 6.45 A.M. we struggled up towards the pass till the line came to an end near the summit, and we were rewarded by some very fine views, exceedingly like those of the Mont Cenis Railway or the Sömmering. The hills on both sides of the line were stippled and flaked with snow, but there was no extensive field, so far as the eye could see, nor was there any appearance whatever of a glacier, the tops generally being clear of snow, which only lodged in the ravines and hollows. Strange it was in these alpine heights to hear the clang of Italian tongues; but most of the navvies were from Italy, and if not quite so strong as English or Americans, they were in more favour with contractors, because they did more work, owing to their steadiness and sobriety. The line was being pushed on at an astonishing rate, and one man was pointed out to us who had laid four and a half miles of railway in one day, " the biggest thing of the kind ever done." Our enjoyment of the scenery was very much diminished by our animal appetites, stimu-

lated by the sharp mountain air, which craved incessantly for food. But not even a cup of coffee was
to be had until we got back to the South Arkansas
station, late in the morning, where an excellent breakfast awaited us. Here we were detained some time by
a derailment of an engine in front.

From South Arkansas station to Leadville (61 miles)
the railroad is still more aspiring. The higher we
ascend the less striking are the scenic effects, but the
grades are not very severe till we come to Malta,
where it reaches 130; from Hilliers to Leadville the
maximum is 176, the curves being often 15°. The
general character of the country may be conceived
from these figures, but no words can convey any idea
of the wholesale destruction of timber which has marked
the progress of the explorers and prospectors. Where
the axe was weary the blaze and the fire were called in,
and hundreds of miles of forest are laid in blackened
ruin. At last we are on a level with the hill-tops.
There, on the hill-tops and in the valleys of a sterile
region in front of you, amidst those tall chimneys
vomiting out smoke and steam, is a wilderness of
wooden huts, " the Great Carbonate Camp"—where we
leave the train—spread out over an undulating plateau,
broken into mound-like hills and sharp hillocks—
bustling streets filled with the most remarkable swarm
of all nations that ever settled on any one spot in
the world. The story of Leadville reads like a
chapter out of some book of Oriental fable. It is a
huge barrack of wooden houses, with some solid and

important buildings, with masses of tree-stumps cropping up in the centre of the main thoroughfares,
pitched over an undulating, rugged, dusty ledge. In
the midst of blocks of houses sprout up the chimneys
of furnaces and mining works, the clang of machinery
fills the air, which is thick with clouds of dust. It was
a few years ago an utterly wild, lifeless waste amidst
the mountains covered with forests, when three
brothers, named Gallagher, exploring from California,
were led by some genius, good or bad, to test the
material of the rocks in the ravine. They struck gold
ore, and silver too, and they set up a claim; and
presently they sold their shares in the land which they
had appropriated, for 40,000*l.*, which they divided.
Two used their wealth wisely, and made more of it,
and, taking to themselves the members of the family,
throve exceedingly ; one, not so wise, if he were quite
as good, did not prosper as well as his brothers. But
the scene of their operations was soon swarming with
enterprising miners. There was a mighty "boom."
Now there is a city! Leadville is, I think, the most
astonishing city on earth, but I am not by any means
inclined to say that it is a place I should like to be
astonished about for more than a few hours.

The party drove to the Morning Star, said to be
the best mine in Leadville ; and the Duke, Lady Green,
Sir Henry Green, and others, went down the mine
in miners' clothes or cloaks. Two others, whose names
I shall not give, remained above, and had, I fancy,
the best of the time. Afterwards we visited Grant's

Smelting Works, and then back to the Clarence Hotel and dined, strolling out afterwards through the town and visiting the billiard saloons, the Grand Central Theatre, and finally, where we were told Leadville life was to be seen in all its glory, the faro and the kino tables, which, however, were doing but very little business, as it was not until after midnight that play in the town generally commenced. Instead of sleeping at the hotel, we resolved to take refuge in the train, which was drawn up at the siding; and we had to drive in order to reach it, as it was considered unsafe to walk through the streets in the dark.

We started at four o'clock next morning, June 18th, and on arriving at Arkansas Station learned that an engine was off the line in front of us. Breakdown gangs were sent for, and all the locomotive talent amongst our passengers repaired quickly to the scene. As it was not easy to lift the engine, the engineers adopted the expedient of laying a temporary rail to turn its flank so as to enable us to pass round it, which we did after a delay of about an hour. The Duke got out and sat on the cow-catcher by way of a change. But the interest we took in the scenery was somewhat diminished by the intelligence that the delay caused by the engine would prevent our enjoying the "soda bath" we had been promised at Cañon City, and the sight of the State Prison, where murderers were to be paraded by the dozen. About twenty miles north of the Grand Cañon, the gorges through which the river runs became wider and deeper. All that has

been written about the Grand Cañon utterly fails to
convey an adequate idea of its exceeding grandeur and
wildness. The rocks—closing in so that the spectator
in the car, looking forward, thinks the progress of the
train must be arrested, and that it is not possible for
it to get out of the *cul de sac* which appears in front,
rising aloft for upwards of two thousand five hundred
feet on each side—are coloured with the brightest
hues, and present an infinite variety of form. The
impetuous current of the Arkansas River, contracted at
times to the breadth of some twenty or thirty yards, and
penned into a space in which the waters boil and toss
as if about to leap on and submerge the passing cars,
roars wildly down below on our right at a depth varying
as the line rises and falls. But it is at the Bridge—a
triumph of engineering skill—that the horrors of the
pass culminate. The sides of the ravine approach so near
that the daring engineer was enabled to execute the idea
of lowering from above a Λ-shaped frame or trestle of
iron; and, the ends catching on each side of the
gorge, permitted him to work on it for the construction of the iron platform over which the train is
carried at a height of some hundreds of feet right
over the maddened river. You can look down through
the interstices of the girders and glance shudderingly
at the hell of waters below—a sight and sensation
never to be forgotten. The ravine gradually expands
and the cliffs recede as the line strikes eastwards; and
though the scenery retains a wild and savage character for many miles farther, the impressions of the

Grand Cañon caused us to regard it with comparative indifference. We heard many tales of the great railway war which was waged for the possession of the pass, of which traces still remained in the ruins of posts of vantage and observation, and the works of the defeated railroad visible on the other side of the ravine. At night we reached Pueblo and took up our quarters in our own cars, and continued our journey, after some delay, towards Kansas City.

CHAPTER V.

KANSAS TO ST. LOUIS.

Liquor Law—Kansas Academy of Science—An Incident of Travel
—A Parting Symposium—Life in the Cars—St. Louis to New
York.

June 19th.—Still on the rolling prairies; in the
country of compulsory abstinence—the paradise of Sir
Wilfred Lawson. At 9.30 A.M. the train stopped at
Newton, 431 miles from Pueblo, and 281 from Kansas.
Here a phenomenon—there was a man by the roadside who walked with unsteady step, whose legs
tottered, and who lurched violently as he came down
the road at that early hour. "He is a sick man,"
observed one of my friends in the train; "that gentleman has been taking *medicine.*" In the Kansas Act
there is a clause enabling physicians, in case of need,
to order stimulants for the patients without penalty;
but I am told the doctors have generally refused to act
upon that permission, so I suppose our friend had been
consulting an unlicensed practitioner.

It would be ill done, when I am anxious to acknow-
ledge the pleasure and profit which I derived from my
passage through the State, if I did not record the
satisfaction with which I perused a volume of the
"Transactions of the Kansas Academy of Science,"

which by accident I picked up at one of the stations.
The very name speaks trumpet-tongued for the progress
which has been made in this wild region. The year
before last, the twelfth annual meeting of the Academy
was held in Topeka, and I find amongst the list of papers
read such subjects as these :—The Kansas Lepidoptera ;
Kansas Minerals ; the Mounds of Southern Kansas ;
Recent additions to Kansas Plants ; Kansas Botany ;
Kansas Meteorites ; Phonetic representations of Indian
Language ; Sinkholes ; Elementary Sounds of Language ; Mound-builders ; On Recent Indian Discoveries. And among the lecturers there was Professor
B. F. Mudge, who died last year, whose name probably is known to a very limited number of scientific
men outside the University of Kansas. Generally the
papers contributed by the gentlemen of the State attest
industry and attainments which make their praise of
the Professor particularly valuable. It is curious
enough to pick up in a railway carriage, traversing
such a scene of comparative wildness and vast unin-
habited plains in Western Kansas, an exceedingly
interesting examination of the Helmholtz theories of
sight. The object of the lecturer would scarcely be
suspected by the reader. We had already been struck
by the extraordinary absence of signalmen, or of any
of the complex apparatus of men and machinery which
may be seen in Europe, and notably in England, to
report the progress of trains on the lines. Collisions,
however, occur in America where these precautions are
not taken, and the lecturer attributed a good deal of

these accidents to colour-blindness, which appears to have attracted considerable attention in the United States. Surgeons, pilots, &c., are tested for colour, and in the army colour-blindness disqualifies the recruit for employment in the signal corps. Altogether the papers give an impression that in this new State there are diligent students of natural history and physics, and profound inquirers into all the phenomena of life. There was a reverse to the medal.

At a station where the train halted beyond Pueblo, a card was handed to me by one of the stewards. " The gentleman is, as he seemed very pressing, outside; but I told him you were engaged." I started as I read the name and address on the card, as well I might. They indicated that an old friend whom I had left in a condition of great bodily weakness and infirmity in London, was close at hand in this remote region—a wonderful if welcome fly in amber. I ran out of the drawing-room into the next car, and there saw a man, agitated and travel-worn, whom I had never, to the best of my belief, seen in my life before. .His story was told, if not soon, at least in time to let me partly understand the situation ere the train moved off. The stranger had been in the service of the gentleman whose card he sent in to me, but had left it to better himself in America, and had gone out as valet to an American of good position at Colorado Springs. He found, however, according to his own account, that he was expected to do things not required of a valet in his own country, such as lumbering, wood-cutting, and the like, and so he had thrown up

his situation and was going back to England. He had
had quite enough of Colorado Springs. " I was not
there above a month, and I was shot at twice," he said.
"Once because I made some remark in a bar-room,
where a chap was abusing Englishmen ; and another
time while I was speaking in the street to a man a
fellow had a grudge against. He fired at him across
the road, and the ball whistled within a hair's-breadth
of my head." He had arrived at Pueblo some time
before our special, and as the morning was warm,
he walked into a bar near the platform, while the
engine of his train was watering, to get a glass of
lemonade. As he was drinking it, a man walked in
and called for a glass of whisky, putting down, at
the same time, what seemed to be a bank note, on the
counter. The boniface said, "I haven't got change
for this twenty-dollar bill—perhaps this gentleman
can oblige you." The unsuspecting Briton, who had
put the money for his passage to Liverpool in a purse,
drew it out to change the note, and the strange
customer at once seized it from his hand, and rushed
off towards the street with his booty. The Britisher
ran after him, but checked his wild career when he
saw, within an inch of his head, the muzzle of a revolver which the robber had drawn, and the fellow
vanished. "Won't you help me to stop the thief ; you
see what has happened?" exclaimed the victim turning
to the barman. " I guess there was no money in that
purse, sir. And if there was, perhaps you had no
more right to it than he had." Then the Briton

dashed off after Don Guzman, shouting "police," and
was at once accosted by an officer of the Pueblo force.
He hurriedly stated the facts. The policeman smiled.
" I think you won't see that pile agin," he remarked ;
" and if you don't look sharp ye'll miss yer train, that's
a fact !" The man had his railway ticket all right, a
few dollars in his pocket, and I told him I would see
him and get him a passage, if I found on inquiry his
story was true. My companions thought the tale sus-
picious—but I believe it was true, and I subsequently
franked the man to England.

Now here we had an exemplification of the manners
and customs of the district. Such an act of violence
and robbery might occur in London—anywhere. But
what of the apathy, or perhaps complicity, of the barman ? And if it or they be considered not altogether
abnormal, is the conduct of the policeman to be accepted as quite consistent with the discharge of a
policeman's duty ? Well, whilst I was pondering on
these things, there came to me the best possible ad-
viser—a judge in this Israel—our excellent Palinurus,
Mr. White. He threw a new, if not a side light on the
subject. "Depend on it he is a confidence man. The
trains are full of them ! Our conductors have express
orders about the rascals." And he explained that a
confidence man is a swindler—very often an Englishman, who makes it his business to look out for unwary
strangers, on whom he imposes with some tale of distress, or some recital of imaginary misfortune and
adventure. As the man I had seen was coming on in

the train in our wake, Mr. White promised to talk with the conductor, and find out, if he could, the truth about the Pueblo robbery. Before dusk a telegram was forwarded by him to me from the station where he left us, to say that the conductor had no doubt the man was robbed, but that it was partly his own fault, and to warn me to be cautious in my dealings with him.

We have now been travelling straight on end for 1160 miles, with only two engineers and two firemen and one engine, a feat of endurance which has greatly exercised the Duke of Sutherland, who, as a practical director of the London and North-Western Railway, has knowledge of such matters, and who contrasts the performance with the experience he has on the home lines, where engines, engineers, and firemen would have been relieved or laid up over and over again. The head engineer of the line, who joined us, Mr. Hackney, formerly of Congleton, had become accustomed to these journeyings and endurances, which were brought to the front in our conversation by the engine-driver appearing at the door of the carriage to claim a dollar which he had won from the Duke in a bet that he could not do the distance without laying up the engine for repairs.

All the long Sabbath-day we travelled on through the prairie, catching glimpses now and then of wooden villages, around which trees were beginning to sprout up, and of the little churches with knots of carts, waggons, horses, and buggies outside, and people waiting for the end of the sermon. Now and then, perhaps at intervals of fifteen miles or so, are places of larger importance, such as Emporia, a rising city on the plains, where many steeples pointed aloft indicated considerable diversity of creed. An authority, not always to be relied upon, stated that there are fourteen churches belonging to the town.

There was a parting symposium in the second Pullman ere we reached Topeka. Mr. White, Major Anderson, General Brown, Mr. Jerome, and my much wandering compatriot, a veritable Irish Ulysses, raised the tuneful melodies of the "Golden Slipper," the "Little Brown Jug," and the other tender psalmodies which had whiled away so many hours, for the last time in our society, and the little gages which were but the outward and visible signs of the regard we felt for our friends were exchanged with honest effusion. There may be—nay, there are—many jealousies and causes of estrangement between the people of the Old Country and of the New, but between the individuals of both there is a *camaraderie* which cannot, I believe, be found between Englishmen and the natives of any country except America.

"Good bye! God bless you! Be sure if ever you come to England you shall have a hearty welcome from me." "And from me!" "And me!" "And me!" The engine bell tolled, and we moved slowly on.

And we were left all alone! The pleasant companions of so many weeks had gone! I wonder if they missed us as much as we missed them?

While travelling across the Rockies and the desert to San Francisco and back, our course of life was pretty uniform, and one day followed another with almost perfect resemblance in the mode of existence and in all things except the scenery and the country through which we were passing. First, in the early morning came one of the attendants to our bedside with a cup of coffee, and then the curtains of the little cubical were thrown aside and you looked out on either plain, or mountain, or river, or col ; and on the faces of early risers at doors or windows as the train passed through some rising town. At one end of the saloon there was a bath-room, and from the tank there was always to be obtained sufficient water for the purpose of an early dip, which was enjoyed as occasion offered in turn by the party. Then a cigarette. Then we dropped in as people do at a country house, into the sitting-room, and exchanged ideas as to the progress made during the night, and the stoppages, wondered where we were, and had a little conversation with the conductor or Arthur as to the place where we could stop or get the papers—and so got over the morning till 9 o'clock, when breakfast was announced, consisting of fish, poultry, meat, fruit (I had nearly said flowers, for there was always a bouquet on the table), tea, coffee, and cold dishes, with abundance of milk and butter. Where the fish came from and how they were kept fresh was matter of wonder, for the instances were very rare in which there was any indication that it had not quite recently come out of the sea or the river. The supply of ice was liberal and unfailing,

and whenever we stopped at any considerable station
the whole disposable strength of the attendants in the
train was employed in grappling with large blocks of
it and stowing it away in the ice reservoir, in which
were the larder and the cellar for such wines as needed
cooling, and for the vegetables and meat, of which there
were great stores constantly laid in. Then after
breakfast there was reading or sight-seeing, investigating the line, examining the maps, receiving visits
and returning them in other parts of the train, till in
the very hot days it was necessary, after expelling the
flies, which were troublesome on occasion, to draw the
dust-blinds and the curtains of the carriages, to mitigate
the fierceness of the sun. It was objected occasionally
that by this process we deprived ourselves of the opportunity of what was called "seeing the country," but
after all a glance now and then is quite sufficient to
reveal the general character of the districts through
which the train is running; and the most diligent and
painstaking observer cannot keep his eyes fixed steadily
for a day on the external aspects of the region through
which he is travelling. I should be sorry to declare
that every one was wide awake all the time of the fore-
noon and up to the period of lunch, which too often
exceeded on the side of many dishes, being, in fact, a
mid-day dinner; but then no one was obliged to eat
more than he liked, or drink either. Then came
the longest stretch of the day, and at its close
another banquet; and as the sun declined and the
temperature decreased, we could take more pleasure in

looking out at the fantastic forms of the vegetation
which clothed the arid rocks in the desert, or on the
bright green prairie, or on the towering mountains,
waiting till the sun had set, generally in a blaze of
glory. There were, of course, interruptions and varia-
tions as we halted at the more important places;
disappointments about letters which had been tele-
graphed for and which were expected day after day,
constituted also a matter of conversation and discourse.
There was an harmonium in the sitting-room of the
palace car, but no one had the art of playing it,
although we had plenty of music of another sort; for
after dinner the gentlemen of the railroad party who
had not dined with us came in, and we were never
tired of listening to the songs, so original and amusing, which they gave with great spirit and admirable
time and tune, for it happened they all possessed good
voices, and the melodies with which the troops of
coloured minstrels have now rendered the world
familiar were then new to us.

During the whole of our tour the weather has been
most favourable. With the exception of the rainy days
in Canada, and the cold and rawness which characterised
the time of our short visit to Richmond, there was
nothing worse to complain of than continual sunshine.
Now and then the temperature was a little too good to
be pleasant when we were traversing the beds of the
dry seas in the desert in Colorado and California, but
that was something to look back upon with satisfaction,
because there was no time lost in keeping within doors

owing to the rain and storm or cold. "Within doors," however, is a phrase scarcely applicable to our mode of life, as it would imply that we were in stable habitations, whereas, as will have been seen by those who have accompanied us so far, we "lived and moved, and had our being" in railway carriages; a mode of life rendered so comfortable by all appliances, that it was sometimes no relief to be told that we would have to pass the night at an hotel.

For nine days and nine nights in succession, on one occasion, we never slept out of the carriages or got out of the train except to take a stroll about the station, or a peep into the street of a small town whilst we were waiting, and one got quite accustomed to that nomad and yet civilised mode of existence, where at every halting-place we were supplied with the latest intelligence by the local papers, and made the recipients of some attention or courtesy, visits and compliments (the remarks of the other sort not being many), bouquets of flowers, presents of fruit, and plenty of conversation. But that my critics might say I dilate too much upon the material enjoyment of life, I would describe at length the means which were supplied in the course of these long journeys for animal enjoyment. Never could there be found more attentive and obliging domestics than the coloured men who waited upon us—Arthur and his fellows. There lived in the kitchen compartment of the train, at the end of one of the saloons, a coloured cook, very intelligent and gossipy, full of quaint conceits and dishes and conversation, who commenced life as a slave on a Southern plantation, probably adopted for indoor purposes on account of his smartness. He liberated himself in the course of the war, and marched off with a regiment of Federals in the capacity of cook and body-servant to one of the officers, wherein he saw a great amount of very hard fighting at very close quarters. This adventurous modern Othello was wont to discourse with much animation when he came out for a breath of fresh air on the platform and could find anybody to talk to him, although he could move no more tender heart than that of Sir Henry Green. The gentlemen of the Atchison, &c., Railway, when travelling with us, had a *cordon bleu* in the saloon—an Italian or Frenchman, I think, or at all events a French-speaking man, who had served also, and would have done credit to an establishment where faults in a *chef* would not lightly be condoned. In the interchange of courtesies, Mr. White and his friends invited our party now and then to dine in the saloon, which was not " across the way," but up a little, on the line, being the saloon in front of us.

But here we are at Kansas City once again! At 5.30 P.M. the train arrived at the platform, which was gay with a Sunday crowd, of whom many were negresses —black, brown, brindled, and yellow *citoyennes*—in much variety of colour and garmenting. Unlike Samson, their weakness is in their hair, and like Achilles, they are vulnerable about the heels (to the arrows of an æsthetical criticism, which accepts the Greek idea of beauty in form); but they seemed to enjoy life amazingly, and not to be in need of beaux; perhaps the happiest people in the world now that their chattel days are over. It was late when we turned into our berths, for it was a lovely night and the fire-flies exercised a great attraction over us, but at last the charm was worn out and we slept till morning without a break.

June 20th.—Still the same boundless plain. In vain does one look for the grass fields with close, even, carpet-like surface to be seen in Europe. We are still passing through exceedingly rich land—the fields covered with flocks of sheep and herds of good-looking cattle. There are more trees by the stream-side, and shrubs growing in the hollows. Habitations are more frequent, and so are fencing and planting. As the sun was setting we approached St. Louis. There were some park-like glades, and vistas opening up to pleasant mansions, amid grounds showing marks of culture. There had been a severe thunderstorm the night before, and the St. Louis Station had still traces of its effects in pools of mud. But the rain had cooled the air, and the people were rejoicing exceedingly in the great improvement that had taken place in the weather, for, they told us, men and women had been dropping down with the heat a few days ago as though they had been struck by musketry.

The appearance of the St. Louis Terminus gave one a high idea of the importance of this city. Eight trains were waiting on their respective lines to start with passengers to all parts of the Union; and by the simple device of placing at the end of each train a large board announcing its destination and the time of its departure, much anxiety was saved to intending passengers, not to speak of the irritation of officials avoided by this simple expedient. The journey was continued by the Indianopolis and Vandalia, and by what is called the "Pa'handle" line to the Pennsylvania Railroad on to Philadelphia. The train was timed on Tuesday so that we were able to see the famous passage over the Alleghany Mountains from Conemaugh to Altoona. For nearly eleven miles we were carried without steam, and with the breaks on, through very fine scenery, down the mountain-side, but the summit was crossed in the darkness of a tunnel 1200 yards long. There are some striking engineering feats in the way of curves and gradients, and the trace of the line is very bold all the way down to Altoona, where the Pennsylvania Railroad engine and machinery shops are established — the centre of a population of some 17,000 souls, where twenty years ago "there were," as a friend· said, "only bears, deer, woodpeckers, and skallywags." The Duke, Mr. Stephen, and our railway experts got out and visited the workshops, and came back very much pleased at the discovery of several London and North-Western men in good positions in the Pennsylvania Railroad Company's service, who welcomed their old directors with effusion, and that there was nothing visible there for Crewe to copy, unless perhaps cast-iron wheels.

The speed at which we travelled was a sensible proof that we were once more on the line of our old friends of Pennsylvania. From Altoona to Harrisburg, 132 miles, we rattled along in two hours and forty-three minutes. On another stretch of the line we travelled eighty-three miles in one hour and forty-two seconds, including stoppages; and the rapid motion was very agreeable, as there was a perceptible increase of temperature after we reached the plains and approached the beautiful valley of the Susquehannah—a scene of industry, prosperity, and peace. Fortunately there was a good light on the river, and we had a fine view of the country all the way to Harrisburg under the rays of the setting sun. A little farther on we were gratified by the appearance of General Roberts at a station on the way, where he was awaiting the Duke to congratulate him on his safe return from the Western expedition, and we bade him farewell at his own house, with many sincere and well-deserved acknowledgments of great and constant kindness. Then over the river by the noble bridge, and on to Philadelphia. We did not visit Pittsburg, which was vomiting out masses of smoke, nor did we halt this time at the capital of the Quaker State.

CHAPTER VI.

NEW YORK—NEWPORT—DEPARTURE.

Coney Island — Newport — Bass-fishing — Habit of Spitting — Brighton Beach—Newport—Coaching—Extra Ecclesiam—Victories of American Horses—Newport Avenues—Return to New York—Our last day in America.

THE special train was detained by the immense amount of traffic on the line, as we approached New York, and we did not reach Brooklyn till a little before 11 P.M. on June 21, so that it was past midnight when we ascended the steps of the Windsor Hotel, which we had selected by way of a change, and found to be every way commendable, with the exception of its distance from the busy parts of the city. The following day was devoted to letter reading and writing, receiving visitors, and various attempts " to go out," which were not generally successful, for New York was palpitating with the intense heat. The " heated term " was in full vigour, but it was now quite temperate in comparison to the excesses which had marked its advent some time before our arrival. In the evening we got up strength and courage enough to go to Wallack's Theatre, a very pretty, well-constructed house, and saw " The World " excellently acted and admirably put on the stage. Next

day, June 23rd, in virtue of a solemn league and
covenant with Uncle Sam and Mr. Hurlbut, the Duke
and I devoted ourselves to fresh fields and pastures new,
and ordered ourselves accordingly for Coney Island.
A long bank of sand by the sea-shore has, by an
accident, become one of the most crowded resorts in the
world, and to-day there were races in the new ground.
It was not, as we found, so easy to get there. Having
the advantage of two experienced guides, our party of
four managed to break up into two and to miss each
other; one taking the boat at one iron pier, and the
other embarking by a different mode of conveyance.
But as we were bound to see Coney Island, the Race-
course being a secondary object, our temporary separa-
tion did not prove a source of great annoyance.

The early settlers would indeed have been astonished
if they could look round and see what they have
brought the quiet place to in these later days. They
were Quakers persecuted by the good Christians of New
England, who were driven out of Boston as ruthlessly
as though they had been malignants and papists of the
worst sort. They settled the township of Gravesend
about 250 years ago, and amongst the conspicuous
settlers occurs the title and name of Lady Deborah
Moody, of whom this deponent knows nothing, but
wonders how, with such a title, she managed to have
influence amongst a Society of Friends.

A ship was built, so the Americans say, of 70 tons in
1699, by the descendants of the Quaker settlers, and less
than 100 years later the bold republicans, abandoning

the doctrines of peace, engaged and captured an English corvette off the island. It was all along of General How, who landed his troops here and set the people to work on the fortifications he threw up, whether they would or no. A corvette, bound to Halifax, anchored off the island, and an old whaler, who, says the chronicler, must have been smarting under the wrongs he had suffered at the hands of the red-coats, or who possibly regarded the work as he would the capture of a finner or a bottle-nose, imparted to a few trusty friends the idea of "cutting her out." So embarking at night in a couple of boats, they stole down with muffled oars and ran up under the stern of the ship. There was no watch, and through the cabin windows the officers could be seen playing cards. The crews of the boats boarded the corvette simultaneously, seized, overpowered, and bound the officers and men, lowered them into their boats, and, having set the man-of-war on fire, pulled over to the Jersey shore with their prisoners. It is to be hoped that the demeanour and language of the captain have been misrepresented by local tradition; but he is said to have cried bitterly, and to have exclaimed, " To be surprised and captured by two blooming egg-shells is too blasted bad ! "

There was a long period of neglect before Fashion and the populace found out the attractions of Coney Island. Fishermen, oyster-catchers, and sportsmen visited the sandy beach from time to time; then after a while a few houses were run up of a very inferior class, and these were frequented by the very worst of the scum of New York, so that it was almost dangerous, and certainly disgusting, to go among them, while the scenes on the beach, to which the present proceedings afford such a contrast, were described as being of the most disgraceful character.

The official directions for spending a day at Coney Island certainly indicate a belief in the possession of enormous physical energy and indefatigable curiosity on the part of the visitors in those who compose the code. Having given you sailing instructions by the iron steamboat to Bay Ridge for the Sea Beach Railway (ticket 35 cents), you are to visit the Sea View Palace Hotel, the Piazza, the two iron piers, the *Camera obscura* (10 cents), the Great Milking Cow, the top of the observatory (15 cents); then to eat a Rhode Island clambake (50 cents), visit the aquarium (10 cents), take a park waggon and ride over the Concourse to Brighton; see the hotel grounds and bathing pavilion there; then take the Marine Railway (5 cents) to Manhattan Beach; visit the Oriental Hotel and take the Marine Railway to Point Breeze (10 cents) and return back to Brighton Beach Pavilion and take a bath; then see the Museum of Living Wonders (10 cents), dine at the Hotel Brighton, hear a concert in the evening, and return to New York by 11 o'clock. "This trip," observes the compiler, "may fatigue one, but the excitement soon overcomes the trouble." Coney Island is indeed an institution.

Along the sea front of the bank for some three or four miles there has been constructed an esplanade lined with seats, and defended from the sea by a stone wall. Outside there is a belt of shingle on which the surf breaks, but not violently, unless in bad weather. Large bathing establishments, with every appliance, are placed at convenient intervals along the shore. Here in the season tens of thousands of people may be seen, all properly and decently attired, disporting in the waves. At the time of our visit, the hour and the season of the year seemed not to be favourable to the indulgence. We were too late in the day. It is an early place, and from 7 till 9 A.M. from the month of June to the end of September are described as the orthodox periods. Nevertheless the spectacle was quite unique, and if you can imagine Brighton with half-a-dozen Pavilions blown out to twice their size, and the largest hotels mutiplied by ten in length, breadth, and depth, you may fancy what the Coney Island front is, provided always that you can also conjure up (literally) myriads of well-dressed men, women, and children perambulating the esplanade or sitting in the grounds around the various establishments which occupy a large space inland—pavilions, hotels, exhibitions, restaurants, and club-houses. There were fireworks going on in broad day ; but these were principally for the purpose of exhibiting very ingenious Japanese figures, which were discharged from bombs, and which gradually descending were objects of eager competition amongst the younger members of the enormous multitude. And with all so much good-humour, so much propriety of demeanour ; none of the

brutal rushes of "roughs" which disgust one with
English popular assemblages—none of the brutal horse-
play, and screams, and unmeaning cries of the 'Arrys
and the Bills of our popular resorts.

Looking at Mr. Marshall's excellent book on the
United States, which we found to be copious and
accurate, I was struck by what he says respecting
a habit of the people which, according to my experience, has very much decreased since I was last
in the States, but which he finds in as full force, and
repulsive as ever. I am bound to say I think the
habit of spitting has very much diminished, but from
numerous evidences, from the presence of spittoons in
every room and in the passages of the hotels, and
from public admonitions, such as one we saw at some
of the theatres, that the audience would not spit upon
the stage, I must believe that it still exists. What
the cause of this habit may be it is not easy to determine. It cannot be in the race, because it is
scarcely an "English" habit. I would be inclined to
attribute it to the drinking of iced water, but ladies in
America use the national beverage quite as freely as
the men, and spitting is a masculine failing. Can it
be a result of climate? Scarcely. For in the States,
British-born people do not seem to be affected by the
influence of the habit in those around them after
many years' residence. Smokers and non-smokers alike
indulge in the practice, so that tobacco cannot be
charged with the disagreeable custom. I assume that
it is as common as Mr. Marshall asserts it is, but

I am bound to say, according to my own observation
and experience on my last visit, that there was no
evidence to show that it was common or national.
Chewing tobacco also appears to me to have fewer
votaries than formerly. A remark to that effect at
Richmond brought upon me something like a rebuke
from the gentleman to whom I spoke, a Judge of the
land. "No, sir," he said, "not at all! I rather think
we chew more than ever!" And, to illustrate his faith,
he produced a silver box, shaped a plug of no doubt
very excellent weed, and thrust it into his mouth. I
do not recollect, however, meeting a gentleman in the
course of our journey who used tobacco in that way,
with that exception.

In the grounds in front of the pavilion, where an
excellent orchestra of some one hundred performers
were playing, sat a very large and appreciative audience,
who applauded with discrimination, and were content
with the good performance of each piece.

Our common rendezvous was the Surf Club, one of
the numerous convivial associations for which Coney
Island seems to be specially adapted; and I presume
the name had nothing at all to do with any supposed
amusements of the members in connection with the
surf on the beach outside. There was some difficulty
in finding our way through a labyrinth of rooms all
filled with guests: with corridors swarming with
people; with vast halls, where at hundreds of tables
there were seated people engaged in the consumption
of the *menu* of a Coney Island restaurant, abounding

in strange dishes and attended by armies of waiters.
At a rough guess, I should say there may have been
about 4000 people in the building—and this was but
one of several—I think the Brighton Beach Hotel,
but of this I am not quite sure.

When the Prospect Park and Coney Island Railroad
was opened none believed in its success, but the fore-
sight of the projector was justified; and when it was
found that respectable people would go there, if the,
vagabonds of both sexes and their associates were
driven away, the police asserted themselves, and swept
off the gamblers and the others of a still more
dangerous class, who were to be found there in
increasing numbers every year; and then hotels were
erected and landing-places made for the steamers;
and now the electric light blazes in a hundred
halls, and music and rejoicing sound late into the
night, contending with the noise of the surf upon the
beach.   Bowling-alleys, shooting-grounds, archery,
croquet, sailing and rowing, all invite some of the
visitors, according to their tastes. An amusing exemplification of the ingenuity of American advertisers is
afforded by the sailing vessels, which display in enormous characters on their main-sails the names of quack
medicines, from which no corner of this continent
appears to be safe.

On June 24th the party, which had been somewhat
dislocated, reunited their scattered forces, and at
2 P.M. started by train after a little repose, for Newport, R.I.   It was a kind of holiday after our travels,

but somewhat out of place, for we were told the
Ocean House was scarcely ready; but we should not
have found it out, had we not been informed of the
fact. The newspapers had been on the alert, and soon
after the Duke's arrival visitors began to call and
invitations to pour in—some well-nigh irresistible, for
they included opportunities for experiences of bass-
fishing.

June 25th.—Newport has not yet put on its festive
attire. It is not the season, and we ought not to be
here. Nevertheless it is. still so pleasant, and so re-
spectably dull, that one enjoys, it amazingly. After
breakfast we walked down to the seashore and sat
gazing on vacancy, and on three yellow ladies collect-
ing clams. Returning thence in a very hot sun, ran to
earth in the hotel where, presently, there were many
visitors; and how kind and anxious to please they
were! Mr. Fearing drove up later on the top of a drag,
and whirled us away to a charming fishing-box on the
shore, in order to judge for ourselves what bass-fishing
was like. It was a very pretty drive, and Mr. Fearing
handled his " four " as if he were bent on joining the
Coaching Club—not indiscreetly, as the horses were
not accustomed to going together, but with satisfactory
decision—and we all were landed without mishap by
the side of the road, close to one of the best-organised
sporting-boxes I have ever seen, built entirely for the
comfort and delectation of Mr. Fearing and two or
three friends who own the bass-fishing stands, at the
end of one of which a gentleman was then busily

engaged in his pastime, for the sea comes rolling up upon the rocks within some forty or fifty yards of the sward of the green meadows on which the house is placed. From it projects into the breakers a platform supported on iron pillars, at the end of which there is an enlargement of the structure to enable the fisherman and his attendants to stand at their ease—the one in hurling the bait and the other in preparing it. And first, as a proof that the labour is not futile, there was exhibited a terrible-headed monster with great scales, which had been caught that morning by Mr. Whipple—a bass of 57 lbs. weight, of which I think the skull and jaws and gills must have weighed a third. The fishing is not, as I found, to be done at once, but needs a little practice. The art of casting consists in the double operation of jerking the bait from the top of a stiff rod, and checking the run of the line without permitting it to overrun, which it is very apt to do in an inexperienced hand, by a pressure of the thumb on the reel, just sufficient to let the weight of the bait carry out the hook to the farthest stretch of the jerk. The rod, not more than eight or nine feet long, a work of great art, and costly, is furnished with a reel, also very expensive, containing a couple of hundred yards of prepared line. At the end is a large single hook, sometimes secured to a piece of piano-wire, as the " blue fish " will cut through the strongest cord or gut. To this is fixed a junk of fat oily fish, of which supplies are kept in a basket close at hand, to be cut up for ever and ever by the attendant, and ever and anon pieces are chucked into the sea, and being of a very unctuous nature, the oil rising to the top, floats away on the surface of the water, and attracts the bass within measurable distance of the platform. Captain Fearing threw, Mr. Whipple threw, and the gentlemen at the end of another pier emulated them, and pounds, perhaps stones, of bait were thrown into the sea, but the bass, which are capricious, like most fish, were not to be caught; and so after a time we returned to the cottage.

I was, unfortunately, unable to accept an invitation from one of the many hospitable gentlemen in Newport, to go out and spend the evening on a desolate island, where they are said generally to have exceedingly good sport, in order to get up before sunrise the following morning and essay my skill, or want of it, in bass-fishing. Mr. Wright, an enthusiastic sportsman, availed himself of a like invitation with great pleasure and with many anticipations of delight, but on Monday morning he returned weather-beaten back, and bootless and bass-less home, although he assured me he enjoyed himself very much, and had very agreeable company out at sea on the rock.

The following day (June 26th) was cloudy and cool, and all that was of rank and fashion in Newport went to All Souls Church. There are many churches in Newport, and in the height of the season, each is, I am told, well filled on Sundays. And wonderful it is that there is neither dissension nor controversy among the congregations. They mingle together coming and going, affording to me, who have been accustomed at times to observe the manners and customs of my country men and women on like occasions in Ireland and elsewhere, ground for wonder, not unintermingled with an ardent desire that we, nearer home, could learn the secret of this moderation.

Mr. Bridgman, our fellow-passenger in the "*Gallia,*" is enjoying his *villeggiatura* with his wife and family in a pretty little cottage. We were very much pleased indeed to renew our acquaintance with him, although there was no scope for the display of his fine talents as a salad-maker. It was not foggy enough for the ladies, who delight in a thick and moist *brume* from the Banks, and who sit at the open windows when it comes on for the sake of their complexions, as it is esteemed a sovereign cosmetic beyond Maydew or Kalydor. Whether it be rightly credited with these virtues or not, I can answer for the presence of many fair ladies in church, and on their way to and fro in the streets. We dined with Mr. and Mrs. Keene, who reside in one of the best villas of the many charming dwellings in Newport.

The victories of the American horses in France and England created an enthusiasm in the States almost as intense as though they had been won by the national fleets or armies. From one end of the Union to the other the news was flashed the same day, and we saw the names of the conquerors in large letters in every newspaper. Unfortunately there came at the same time reports of foul play to American competitors at the hands of some English roughs, and there was a good deal of heat caused by the objections taken to the entry of the " Cornell Crew " at Henley. These international contests should be very carefully conducted and judiciously worked, or they will do more harm than good, if indeed they do any good at all. The injurious insinuations respecting the age of Foxhall could but excite indignation in the minds of honourable men against whom they were directed.

There is a State House in the town, and there is also a mansion occupied by Commodore Perry, but the most useful inhabitant of the place appears to have been one Abraham Touro, a Jew, who gave his name to the park, a cemetery, a synagogue, and a street. Altogether there is rather an old-world air and look in the town; but one must go along the Avenues to have an idea of the charms which lead so many of the principal families of the Eastern States to make the place a resort when they are not enjoying the delights of travel in Europe, or that blissful existence which endears Paris to our Transatlantic relatives. Bellevue Avenue is bordered by a number of very sprightly dwellings, of every order and disorder of architecture, and rejoicing in all the extraordinary richness and elaboration of American workmanship in wood, each standing in a little park of its own, generally rich with trees, shrubs, and an ornamental garden. Several of these interiors, as we had reason to know, were furnished in the very best taste, and filled with objects of art, excellent examples of good masters, principally foreign, and articles imported from all the corners of the globe. Of an afternoon the ladies might be seen driving, in very well turned-out carriages, to some rendezvous where lawn-tennis or a picnic awaited them; and altogether, even at this time of year, Newport presented a picture of great refinement and comfort, which enable the visitor to understand how attractive it must be in the height of the season, and why it is Americans are so fond of life in Rhode Island.

I am not in a position to throw the smallest doubt upon the statement that the mass of stones in the form of a tower, ivy and moss covered, and evidently the work of human hands, was not built by the hardy Norsemen hundreds of years before the arrival of Columbus. There are, moreover, people who declare that the erection is due to a British governor of the colony, when it was more prosperous as a commercial resort, though not so fashionable as it is at present. But American antiquaries take a great pleasure in propping up the proofs which have been adduced of Scandinavian enterprise and discovery on the continent, many centuries before Vespuccius, Columbus, and the English navigators lived.

We dined on the evening of the 27th at the house of Mr. Shattock, a gentleman of New York, who had assembled a party of very pleasant people to meet the Duke, and kindly hastened his dinner-hour to suit our convenience, as we were obliged to go on board the Fall River boat, which called at 9.30 P.M. to take

up passengers for the Empire City. There was some
difficulty about getting cabins or state rooms as they
are called, but "Uncle Sam," who came from New
York to consort with us quietly, applied himself
diligently to telegraph wires, telephones, and the like,
and when the great steamer came alongside the wharf
our dormitories were ready. The night was calm and
fine. There was an excellent band, quite worthy of
being called an orchestra, on board, which played to
the delight of a large audience till it was bed-time.
As a "sight" for a foreigner, nothing could be more
striking than the vast saloon, brilliantly illuminated,
with hundreds of people on sofas, chairs, and benches,
reading or conversing in the intervals of the music,
and presenting infinite varieties of type and class, yet
all so orderly and well-behaved; and if you moved
quietly through the crowd, your ear caught many
strange languages interpolating the American speech
—German, French, Polish, Russian, Italian, and, perhaps the natives would say, British. There is some
care observed in the locking up of cabins, and I believe
there are detectives and police on board the boats;
but it is said they do not look after the morals of the
passengers, and concern themselves only with vested
interests in portable property. There was no sea on,
and the only motion was caused by the beating of the
paddles and the throbbing of the engine, and early in
the morning of the next day we were at our quarters
in our comfortable hotel in the Fifth Avenue.

June 29*th.*—And yet more excursions. Bound by

a long-standing engagement, a small detachment of our
party set out this evening to visit Mr. Barlow at his
country place, Long Island, which travellers, perhaps,
have not much occasion to see. The Mayor of New York
(Mr. Grace) and Mr. O'Gorman were on the steamer
which took the Duke, Mr. S. Ward, Mr. Hurlbut, and
our host down the Sound, and were introduced to us
by Mr. Barlow. The first-named gentleman I mentioned in one of the early pages of this diary in connection with the vigorous efforts to purify the civic
atmosphere made by him on his accession to office. I
learn that he has since obtained a large measure of
success, and let me hope corresponding thanks from
his fellow-citizens. Attacks on corrupt influences are
apt to receive lukewarm support from the politicians.
The power of the respectable classes, which hold aloof
from politics, is not large. Mr. Grace had more opposition than help from his own countrymen, who have
been long nearly omnipotent in New York, and who
monopolise a large proportion of the civic offices and
employment. Mr. O'Gorman, one of the traversers
with O'Connell in the famous State trials, is one of the
leading lawyers of New York, and is held in much
respect by his fellow-citizens. The "old Country" is
still dear to him, but I seemed to gather from his
remarks that he shared in the distrust which American
lawyers generally expressed respecting the principle of
the Land Bill then under discussion as far as interference with the law of contract—"the very foundation of social life"—was involved. Glen Cove is

a beautiful place, standing high above the level of
the sea, and commanding charming views of the
sound and of the opposite shore. It is surrounded
by trees, ornamented by woodland and fine natural
groves, broken up by ravines, through which trickle
streams of water. The mansion is furnished with
every comfort and luxury, and we had a garden to
saunter about in the morning, and a genial hostess to
talk to, and her fair daughter to sing for us, so that
it would have pleased us well to have made a longer
sojourn at Glen Cove. Here we passed two very
peaceful days, part of Wednesday and Thursday, and
in a pleasant drive with our host in the early morning had some slight outlook on umbrageous Long
Island. *"O! si angulus iste!"* It is 115 miles long
and 14 miles broad, and quite big enough for me!
And there be deer in the woods and trout in the rivers,
and fish in all the creeks, and game in the wooded
lagoons, and forest, lake, and civilised life, and many
things to please the eye; and then the comet was so
good as to display his glories and his tail before
Glen Cove. But our time of departure from the States
was drawing near, and there were still things to be
done in New York, and many engagements to be kept,
ere we started on our homeward journey on July 2nd;
and at 12.35 on the 30th June the Duke and I took
the "cars" at a rural station, and reached New York
at 2.35, in time for a run through Tiffany's and some
little shopping and visiting. There was a dinner
arranged by "Uncle Sam" at "Sutherland's" in

honour of the famous city restaurant. The house is one of a type which has, I believe, disappeared in the " City," where once flourished famous establishments such as Williams' Beef Shop in the Old Bailey, Dolly's in Paternoster Row, the Billingsgate Fish Ordinary, Jacquet's, &c., like it in character. Great New Yorkers do not disdain to cross the threshold, within which they find admirable fare and excellent wines—the national delights of clam chowder, clam soup, soft-shell crabs, and many other Transatlantic delicacies—at the far end of Broadway, still holding its own against the fashionable restaurants. Of the party who dined there with Chancellor Robertson and others in 1861, only " Uncle Sam," Mr. S. Barlow, and I survive ; but the host, a granitic sort of man, with a kindly Scottish heart warming the case inside, seems capable of presiding over his feasts for another generation.

July 1st.—It was difficult to realise the idea that this was our last day in America, but the truth was forced on us by the practical duties of getting the baggage ready and settling up generally, ending with a dinner at the Turf Club, where we met Mr. Keene, of Foxhall fame, who had also entertained us at Newport, Mr. Jerome, Mr. Stuart, Mr. Travers, and other fathers of the New York sporting world, which seems very like our own, and had to drink madeira of all but fabulous antiquity and excellence.

CHAPTER VII.

RETURN TO EUROPE.

The " *City of Berlin* "—The Inman Line—The Service at Roche's
Point—Queenstown Discomforts—A sorry Welcome Home.

July 2nd.*—Up at 5.30. The Duke, Lady Green,
Sir Henry, Mr. Wright, Edward, all engaged in the
transport department, with Mr. Trowbridge in observation; incessant activity. The Queen Anne coach
was in readiness at 7.30, and in half an hour more we
were discharged at the Inman wharf. There was
a great flotilla—five large steamers leaving at the
same period for Liverpool, and there was the usual
throng at the landing-places of friends to bid "good-
bye" to those who were about to cross the Atlantic.
The steamer we had selected belonged to the Inman
line, and whatever there may have been wanting to
the eye on board, compared to the trimness and paint
of the Cunard steamers, there was nothing to regret

---

* The day of our departure from the United States, after the visit
of which I have been giving the details, was the date of a great crime,
of which we were then ignorant. About the very time that we were
on our way to the wharf to embark on board the " *City of Berlin*," the
murderer of the President was accomplishing his purpose. But with
all the means and appliances which exist for the despatch of news,
I believe that the commission of the crime was not known till the
steamer had passed out to sea from the Sand Heads.

in our accommodation or service. There were so many
passengers that the dining-saloon, illuminated by the
electric light—which was also used for the purpose of
lighting the engine-room and the lamps in the
corridors—would not contain them all at the same
time, and so there were two messes for dinner. Epergnes
filled with the most beautiful flowers were ranged in
order, and a rampant war-steed composed of white
roses was displayed on the table. I am not about
to give a log-book, or to trespass on the patience of
my readers by an account of such an ordinary event
as a passage home. The second day after we left New
York was the anniversary of Independence, July 4th,
and the day was duly celebrated by the citizens of the
United States, who constituted the large majority of
our fellow-passengers. The " stars and stripes " were
hoisted at the main, and the cabin was draped with
British and American flags. But there was no
speechifying, and the spread-eagle was content with
moderate flights; a recitation and a song or two, and
the fire of champagne corks, being the only indications
of an extraordinary festivity.

About this time of the year the Atlantic, in the lati-
tudes which we traverse, is rather vexed of fogs; and
if one be disposed to low spirits, I know nothing which
weighs upon him more than the sound of the fog-horn.
But what must it be for the captain, who is perforce
obliged to go at full speed, or as near to it as he
can, with the expectation every moment of some startled

cry from the bow "Sail right ahead!" Nor is it quite out of the running that an iceberg may be taking a sail across his course. Fortunately we had no experiences of the kind; and as night was falling on the 10th July land was in sight.

The lights of the Fastnet were seen through drifting haze, and about 10 o'clock at night the "*City of Berlin*" steamed through a rising sea, with a strong beam wind, into the roadstead of Roche's Point, burned her rockets, and laid-to for the steamer to take the mails, and those passengers who had decided to land, on shore.

It was blowing freshly, and rain fell heavily; and as we looked down from the lighted decks on the murky water, and made out the tug as she paddled up to us, rising and falling on the waves, we were seized with reasonable misgivings as to the propriety of leaving our ship and taking to such a craft. I am bound to say that our experience more than amply justified them.

I am writing these lines with a very faint hope that any amendment will be introduced, in consequence of what I say, into the abominable service between the American vessels off Roche's Point and Queenstown. In fine weather and in daylight it is not of much consequence, perhaps, what discomfort one may be exposed to in a short passage to the shore; but to affront women and children with the misery which must be experienced at night time and in bad weather, in the steamers employed in the service, is little short of barbarous, if it be not indeed altogether so.

After I had got down upon the deck of the little steamer and surveyed the scene around me, I thought that it would have been much wiser to have gone on with my friends to Liverpool; but I had some engagements in Ireland, and so had the experience I was glad not to share with my fellow-passengers, on whom I should have liked the old country to have made a favourable impression. There was the great steamer, with hundreds of waving hands, and the sound of friendly voices bidding us "God speed," a blaze of lights, and almost as steady as the solid earth, as the horrible little tug puffed away, and, getting from under her lee at once, encountered the swell. If she could have ridden over the water below, she certainly could not escape that which came down from above; so that we were all pretty wet and cross and miserable in the half-hour which elapsed before we reached the shore. Fortunately, there were not many passengers who availed themselves of the opportunity; but the deck of the steamer was crowded by poor people returning to their native country. Accommodation for the cabin passengers, except seats on the wet and sloppy decks, there was none. There was a little cabin, stuffy and comfortless, and moreover occupied by a couple of women who had come out to see friends by way of a pleasure excursion, and who were suffering the last extremities of sea-sickness. The spray broke over the luggage and passengers; it was in such circumstances that the custom-house officers began their search. One of them, opening my bag, which was unlocked, found a small revolver. It was unloaded, and there was no ammunition for it; but, nevertheless, it was seized, for I was "importing arms into a proclaimed district without licence." A similar mishap occurred to a Spanish officer, who was not quite so easily appeased as I was by the assurance that the arm would be given up on proper application to the police. His revolver, he insisted, was part of his uniform, a necessity of his existence, and the authorities might as well seize his epaulettes or spurs. However, my deadly weapon was restored to me some days afterwards, after a correspondence with the custom-house, and I dare say the Hidalgo was equally fortunate. These were incidents to denote that we were in the midst of trouble. There was but a sorry welcome for us when we landed at Queenstown. Not a car to be found, that I could see; but there were a few porters, and the agent of the hotel at the pier; and, commending my luggage to his care, I walked to the establishment. It surely cannot be quite an unaccustomed event for a steamer to arrive at Queenstown at that time of night! The last train for Cork had gone; and it might have been expected that lighted rooms and some sort of preparation would have awaited the travellers; for every vessel that touches at Queenstown, coming from America, surely lands a few people needing rest and refreshment? A demoralised waiter, who appeared to think that such a thing had never happened in the whole course of his experience, as the inroad of ten or twelve people asking for supper and bedrooms, informed us that nothing could be done until the gentleman who represented the hotel at the landing-place had arrived; and so we sat on the stairs for half an hour, and were then shown into a gaunt room, dimly lighted by gas. There was nothing ready. The hungry people, by dint of patience and perseverance, eventually succeeded about midnight in obtaining some poor substitute for supper and scrambled to their beds.

I mention the circumstances in which my fellow-passengers and I were landed at Queenstown, that those who are interested in promoting the welfare of the port, and in making the route through Ireland less thoroughly objectionable, may take steps to obviate the great inconvenience to which travellers at present are certainly exposed.

Next morning I reached Mallow. I was but a few hours in the "distressful country," but I found that things had gone from bad to worse while we were in the States. I heard from my fellow-travellers in the train that "Boycotting" had attained such a pitch in the South, that all the relations and conditions of social life were exposed to peril, if not destruction. And still, with the usual cheerfulness of Irish landlords, accustomed, as it were, to these excesses of the popular will, my informants talked of hunting, fishing, and shooting; and I heard full accounts of the state of

the rivers, and of the take of fish which had made some
of them happy. The County Cork, indeed, had nearly
a parallel in the " wild West." But what a contrast
between the state of public feeling, in respect to the
outrages which were perpetrated in each, in the country
we had left, and that to which I had returned! In
the United States there was no attempt to justify the
men who were guilty of such deeds. In Ireland it
was impossible to obtain evidence or to convict the
offenders. I am not going to close this narrative of
our little excursion with a political disquisition, indeed
I have not the materials for forming any opinion respecting the breadth and depth of what may be called
the Irish national movement in the United States;
but there seems to be a general vague impression in
America that as the British Government was not very
wise and equitable in its dealings with the people of
the thirteen colonies in the reign of King George, it
is, somehow or other, at the present moment, treating
with harshness and injustice the whole of the Irish
race in Ireland. It is impossible not to recognise the
fact that the head, perhaps the heart, and certainly
the purse of this development of Irish discontent are in
the United States. The arms, the body, and the legs
are in Ireland. During the whole time of our visit,
although we visited towns where eminent orators were
lecturing upon Irish subjects, and where representatives of the League were in session, there was not a
trace brought home to us of the strong sympathy which
undoubtedly exists in many American cities with the

movement in Ireland. There were accounts of the meetings in the newspapers, and now and then a few leading articles on the subject; but we might have concluded, from what we saw and heard generally, that the Irish question was of far less importance to the American people than the religious views of Colonel Ingersoll, or the discussions between the railway companies respecting their fares. The recital of wrongs, most of which have been long ago redressed, still reaches the ear and touches the heart of the American public, and if the Irish population had not in many ways provoked or excited the antagonism of the native Americans in the towns, and of the Teutonic element which exercises such a powerful influence in the country, there would be far greater sympathy for the supposed oppression of the Sister Island by England. The fact that emigrants come from Europe is accepted as a proof that the countries which they leave are ill-governed; and Americans, in dealing with the emigration question, are apt to forget the existence and nature of the forces which induced their own ancestors to seek homes in the New World.

The *New York Times* declared in an article last June, that there is no essential difference between the two divisions of the Irish in America and of the Irish in Ireland. The voyage across the Atlantic works no transformation in Pat, and he is still as much an Irishman after his plunge into an alien civilisation and taking out his papers as when he stood on the old sod in Meath or Tipperary. " He cares no more for

the American eagle than for an owl; but a sprig of
shamrock stirs him to ecstasy. The name of Washington has no meaning for his ear; but that of St. Patrick
is a living and potent reality." That statement, however, must be taken with qualification. There are
to-day 90,000 acres of land in Minnesota as thoroughly
Irish as if they were planted in the centre of Con-
naught. There are Pats and Pats. Many of the
most wealthy and prosperous merchants, bankers, and
landowners whom we met in the West were not merely
of Irish extraction, but born Irishmen, and the extraordinary spectacle of Irish millionaires who knew how
to keep their money, and to add to it, too, may be seen
in San Francisco and elsewhere in the West. Many,
less fortunate, have high positions either in the army, or
as politicians, or in the estimation of all that is great
and good in America—such as Mr. O'Conor—men who
have held aloof from politics, and who could not be
tempted, even by the Presidentship, to enter the arena
of party strife. One convicted rebel of 1840 now
occupies a leading place at the American bar. I heard
him denounce the Land Bill in terms he might have
used in denouncing the atrocities of the Saxon in his
hot days when O'Connell was king. The influence
which has been acquired in many parts of the Union
by the Irish immigration and by the descendants of
immigrants has naturally excited at various times the
opposition and indignation of the American born, and it
has always been more or less opposed by the Teutons
of different nationalities who occupy such a powerful

position in all the great States of the West. But "the
Native Party" is now either dead or sleeping. A very
distinguished officer and politician said to me that he had
at one time been a most eager and ardent adherent of.
the policy of the Native American Party, but that when
he saw how earnestly and devotedly the Irish had come
forward in defence of the Union, how brilliantly they had
fought, and how recklessly they had sacrificed their lives,
in 1861, he felt constrained to abandon his principles,
and to admit their free right to all the privileges of
American citizenship. I could not, however, but recollect that General Richard Taylor, in his most
amusing, able, and graphic work on that same war,
from the Confederate side of the question, bore the
strongest testimony to the services of the Irish in the
army which fought under the banner of the Slave
States. In New York and in San Francisco the Irish
element has exercised almost supreme control in municipal matters, and it may be said, without offence I
hope, that, whether it be owing to the opposition they
have encountered or to a radical deficiency which may
be Irish rather than Celtic, their management has
not conduced to the comfort of the cities or to the
pecuniary purity of the Executive. In San Francisco
there is a strong anti-Irish press and much anti-
Irish feeling. The 'Argonaut' repudiates the thraldom
of the Irish associations and factions in the Far West
as strenuously as the 'Times' and 'Tribune' do in the
East. But notwithstanding all that may be written
and done, it is impossible to resist the influence of

numbers under a system of suffrage so large as that which exists in the greater number of the American States. It was curious to read in a Californian paper an appeal to England to suppress Irish agitation. "We confidently believe," says the *Argonaut*, "that the wisdom of its public men, the healthful condition of its public opinion, and the strength of its military power will be sufficient to crush out the Land League movement, which is but incipient rebellion. That England will deal justly, firmly, and successfully with this effort of united ecclesiasticism and Communism is the earnest wish of every intelligent and independent mind that believes in free government, the guarantees of property, the rights, and the personal liberty of man." However, there are American parties, if not statesmen, whose wishes are by no means directed to such a consummation, and we must take note of the fact.

CHAPTER VIII.

SOME GENERAL REFLECTIONS.

Education—Free Schools—Influence of Money in Politics—Corruption in Public Life—Crime on the Western Borders—The Great Rebellion—Anniversaries—Great courtesy to strangers—Manners and Customs.

> " Westward the course of Empire takes its way ;
> The four first acts already past,
> A fifth shall close the drama with the day,
> Time's noblest offspring is the last."

THE "tar-water Bishop of Cloyne" would have been exceedingly astonished could he have seen the first line of his prophecy or averment made to do duty as a motto to Mr. Bancroft's History of the United States ; but surely if the prophecy be not realised, it will be the fault of the agencies engaged in working it out— never in the history of mankind, as we know it, have such advantages been enjoyed by any nation as have been, and are, the appanage of the Americans of European origin in the New World. They have leaped into the possession of their heritage full armed, like Minerva from the brain of Jove. For them have all the champions of human rights died or conquered, and the protagonists of human struggles for liberty and light fought. For them Science has trimmed her

lamp—for them martyrs have died—for them Europe
and Asia have been in toil and travail for countless
generations, and they have been guided across the
sea to a grand continent where it would seem as if
Nature had been engaged for myriads of ages to provide for their happiness and grandeur—all climes and
all products are theirs—the bounteous plain, the ore-
filled mountain, the treasures of the deep, the heaven-
made ways by lake and river, and it would be a
despair for all mankind if they misuse their glorious
inheritance, and if all the nations of the world see
that the pillar of fire in the west was but an *ignis
fatuus* dancing before their aching eyes in a Serbonian
bog of creeds and 'isms, of factions and faiths, all
struggling towards the gate of the Temple of Mammon. "Philosophers," in all the doubts and fears
which the condition of the Republic inspires at times,
cling with confidence to the palladium which is, they
think, to be found in the system of education based
on the free schools of the States. If there were not a
distinction between knowledge and morality, they
would be justified ; but the Evil One tempted us to
eat of the fruit of the tree which brought sin into the
world, and if Americans are to be trusted as authorities,
the result of the largest and most liberal system of
education ever devised is not as happy in practice as
it ought to be according to theory.

As the central Government extended its sway over
the Territories there was a uniform system, when as-
signing land for public objects to railway companies, of

retaining for the School Fund a portion of the land in each Territory, as it was settled and admitted as such, under the control of the central Government. In the States Constitutions creating Sovereign States, there are provisions inserted, varying very little in language and not at all in spirit, which render it compulsory on the Legislature of each State to maintain public schools free to all the children of the people residing within its borders. Another principle, of universal application, provided that all schools under public control should be free from sectarian or denominational teaching, in the schools or in the books used for educational purposes. With such safeguards for the extension of education, it is depressing to find that, in certain districts at all events, crime and immorality prevail in the United States as extensively as in the benighted kingdoms of the Continent of Europe. But the most serious consideration in connection with the system of common schools in America, is the fact that serious doubts are intruding themselves respecting the success of it. In a recent official report it was stated that whereas the children who ought to go to school numbered about fourteen and a half millions, the average attendance was not more than five millions. But, assuming that all the children went to school, there are people who declare that the education given under the National system is by no means satisfactory. Mr. R. G. White affirms that the system is a failure; and high authorities assert that " any comparison between the results obtained in the public schools of

New York, Cincinnati, and Boston, with those of such public grammar schools of England, as Bedford, Manchester, and the City of London, is simply ridiculous." The teachers are continually shifting, and when the teachers, as they do in this land of liberty, go away, the schools are deserted, the constant services of a staff cannot be retained unless there is very considerable increase in the rate of payment now made to the male and female teachers. None of these in any State have, I think, more than about 9*l.* per month. Mr. White says that " the mass of the pupils of the public schools are unable to read intelligently, to spell correctly, to write legibly, to describe the geography of their own country, or do anything that reasonably well educated children do with ease; and they cannot write a simple letter, they cannot do readily a simple sum in practical arithmetic, they cannot tell the meaning of any but the commonest of words they read and spell so ill. They can give rules glibly, they can recite from memory, they have some dry knowledge of the various ologies and osophies, they can, some of them, read a little French or German with very bad accent; but, as to all real education, they are as helpless and as barren as if they had never crossed the threshold of a schoolhouse." It is from American writers that these accusations against the common school system are to be gleaned. Some statisticians say that crime and pauperism are increasing far more rapidly than population. The charge on the State for punishing criminals and keeping paupers last year was $20,000,000, or

£4,000,000 ; but it is too much to attribute crime and pauperism to the defects of the schools. It might with more reason be argued that the teaching of the people in the schools tends to develop the looseness and eccentricity of thought, where there is no religious teaching, which are exemplified in the uprising of extraordinary sects and strange philosophies ; for America is the land of spiritualists, mesmerism, soothsaying, and mystical congregations. Mr. Hepworth Dixon may not be a perfectly unimpeachable authority on the subject of the number of spiritualists in America ; but there can be no question they are to be counted by millions. It is averred that believers in spirits generally believe in " special affinities which imply a spiritual relation of the sexes higher and holier than that of marriage." It is not wonderful then that there should be also a very large number of divorces, especially in the New England States. Mr. Nutting says that " in the history of nations there has never but thrice occurred such a breaking up of the family tie as is now taking place, especially in Rhode Island and Connecticut, among the people of New England blood." Mormonism, although of American origin and early growth, has been mainly successful by the constant importation of ignorant peasants from Europe.

There is a want of reverence on the part of children towards their parents which is very striking. Americans who have admitted and deplored this have sought to account for it by the school system, wherein the

State usurps the place of the parent, and teaches the young idea to mock at any authority but that of the schoolmaster. It would be lamentable to have to admit that free education is associated with the weakening of parental influence. Theoretically, there is nothing in the American system to prevent the teaching of religious and moral duties by parents at home ; but it would seem as if very little of that kind of instruction was given by the busy fathers and anxious mothers of the Republic, and that when the day's work is done at school, and some time given to the preparation of the studies for the day to follow, there is no further teaching.

I do not think the rule " By their fruits shall ye know them " can be applied to the public schools, in connection with the prevalence of crime, immorality, unbelief, or eccentric religion. But it is certain the system has not by any means secured that high level of general education, or what education is supposed to bring with it, which its friends claim for it in the States. There is reason to believe that the standard of morality has not been uniformly high in the political world, and that in the public intelligence the judiciary does not aspire to an absolute immunity from suspicion. Even in the old settled States, legislators from time to time may be found, who, seated among the good and wise, excite admiration akin to that which is aroused by the spectacle of a fly in amber. It has been observed by travellers that whatever affection

may exist in families, it does not attain that keen
sensibility and lasting power which is found in French
domestic life.

When American newspapers of the greatest influence
and circulation write invectives against the corruption
which prevails in places high and low, when writers
of great intelligence and known character contribute
similar articles to periodicals which possess the highest
position in the literary world of America, a stranger
may be permitted perhaps to say a few words respecting the impression produced upon his mind by what
he heard and read on the subject when he was in the
country, without it being alleged that he attemps to
assail the principles of free government, or to make
invidious charges or wholesale accusations against a
nation. I know too well the force with which Americans could retort if they were so minded, and how
they could point to the reports of election judges
which set forth the prevalence of extensive bribery,
led to the suspension of writs, and will perhaps end in
the disfranchisement of some ancient and populous
boroughs and constituencies in England, and to the
speeches of Sir Henry James in Parliament, to cast
any stone out of my glass house on that score ; but I
do not think it can be established that persons in a
position at all analogous to that of the members of
a State Legislature have been purchased wholesale in
England, Ireland or Scotland, or that even a complete
Borough Corporation had been bought up. Now,
nothing was more common in the Far West than to

hear it stated openly that Senator So-and-so had
bought his place, and that Mr. So-and-so had purchased a State Legislative body in order to "get
through" some railway or other scheme. That was
accepted in fact as a matter of course, and not con-
tradicted or questioned by any one. We heard from
time to time of the sums which So-and-so would
expend to buy his senatorship, and of the money
actually paid to secure the passage of a line from the
legislature of O—— and the like, whilst stories relating
to the purchase of judges were common in the conversation of the hotels and cars.

I do not aver that these stories were true. I only
know that they passed current and were not challenged
by those who were around us. "Thoughtful persons,"
who exist in the United States as well as in the
vicinity of Pall Mall clubs, lament, deplore and hate the
evils of growing corruption with all the fervour of
honest and powerless natures. The mechanism is
scarcely concealed. It stands before the world with less
attempt at disguise than the gallows in the gaol. Mr.
Parton, in the 'North American Review' of this July,
writing on the power of public plunder, says: "At
present, in the ninety-fifth year of the Constitution,
we are face to face with a state of politics of extreme
simplicity, of which money is the motive, the means and
the end. What was the last Presidential election but a
contest of purses? The longest purse carried the day,
and it carried the day because it was the longest.
Some innocent readers perhaps have wondered why the

famous orators who swayed vast multitudes day after
day and night after night, have not been recognised in
the distribution of office. They were paid in cash from
ten dollars a night to a thousand dollars a week." And
then he goes on to describe the business in detail, and
to show what this power is. He says: "There is a
boss in the city of New York who will take a contract
for putting a gentleman into Congress. Pay him so
much and you may go to sleep, wake up and find your-
self member elect. A boss is a man who can get to
the polls on election days masses of voters who care
little or nothing for the issues of the campaign and
know of them still less. They operate upon the
strangers in the land who are unable to use its
language and are unacquainted with its politics."
Mr. Parton describes with humour one of these
"bosses," an improvement on the pugilists and cor-
morant thieves of a remote period. " The Emerald Isle
gave him birth; the streets of New York, education.
To see the brawny, good-tempered Irishman walking
abroad in his district when politics are active is to get
an idea of how the chief of a clan strode his native
heath when a marauding expedition was on foot. He
lives in a handsome house, and has more property than
any man has ever been able to get by legitimate service
to the United States. He treats his dependants and
retainers nobly, but as the agent and organiser of
spoliation he is a prey to every minor scoundrel, for
at certain seasons he dare not say no to any living
creature. And yet it requires tact, self-possession

and resource to move about among needy people with
a pocket full of money, an embodied "yes," and have
some of it left after the election.   The strikers, as
they are called, go for solid cash now instead of target
companies and clambakes for which the candidates
paid the bills." "Money, money," exclaims Mr. Parton,
"everywhere in politics, in prodigal abundance, money,
except where it could secure and reward good service
for the public, hecatombs for the wolves, precarious
bones for the watchdogs."   The details in the article
are precise, and if they are to be trusted it may be
doubted whether the claims of the United States to
possess a cheap government can be maintained, for it
is not cheap to pay responsible executive officers a
precarious pittance per annum if now and then it costs
a million dollars to change them.   Mr. Secretary Blaine
has thrice declared that the election in October 1880
in the State of Maine, a model New England State,
was carried by money.   His opponents declared that
he and his party were as bad, and that they too
flooded the towns with money.   What renders the
situation more dangerous is the fact that the men who
provide the money for running these enormously expensive political combinations are either seekers after,
or holders of, office, and the inference is that they seek
to control Government, or, as Mr. Parton puts it, that
"the Government is coming to be rather an appendage
to a circle of wealthy operators than a restraint upon
them."   That is indeed a serious proposition, and the
result of observation goes to support the idea that it

is valid. The small man is in office, but the big man, his master, is outside. The mischief is brought prominently forward in connection with the sale of public lands in the North-West, which have been claimed as the heritage of the people, and indeed of all the nations of the world. The government land attracted the hardy labour of all countries, covering the western west with thriving towns and populous counties. But now the prairies are skinned by rich men, by " land-grabbers," people who buy up tracts of twenty thousand or thirty thousand acres wherever they can lay their hands upon them, evading the law and filling the western world with roving labourers who work on these prodigious farms in summer and starve in winter. This is, we are told, the result of " government by lobby."

Occasionally there is an exceeding great and bitter cry over all this from the depths of the body politic. Some great paper in a moment of deep mental agony publishes an article like that, to which I have called attention, by Mr. Parton; occasionally some preacher. nobly daring, thinks it necessary to direct attention. from his pulpit, to the progress of corruption. Dr. Talmage delivered a very remarkable discourse whilst I was in America on the text from Job. xv. 34: " Fire shall consume the tabernacles of bribery." Although I do not profess exactly to understand to what particular sect he belongs, he is one of the leaders of religious thought, dividing with Beecher and others the popular favour in the Empire City. The State buildings at Albany ought to be heavily insured if the reverend gentleman's vaticinations are right. It was an American discourse. I cannot give the whole oration. The people of the Brooklyn Tabernacle were presented with a muster-roll of the people who had distinguished themselves amongst the great ones of the world. Cobden, Brougham, O'Connell and Rowland Hill were placed in juxtaposition as leaders on our side of the water. Of course it was impossible to resist the allusion to Francis Bacon and to Macclesfield; but it was scarcely correct to say that the Lord Chancellor Whiteberry—I presume a misprint for Westbury—"perished," nor do I quite understand what the preacher meant by the awful tragedy of the *Credit Mobilier.* Washington, Ben Butler, and John McClean were linked together for the benefit of Americans. They were, Dr. Talmage declared, great politicians, but "out of politics there has come one monstrous sin, potent and pestiferous, its two hands rotten with leprosy, its right hand deep in its breeches pocket. This is bribery." Dr. Talmage called upon the American people to judge the crime. "Under the temptation of this sin," he exclaimed, "Benedict Arnold sold the fort in the Highlands for thirty-one thousand three hundred and seventy-five dollars; Gorgy betrayed Hungary, Ahitophel forsook David, Judas killed Christ. I think," he says, "when I see the strong men who have gone down, of the Red Dragon in Revelation, having seven heads and ten horns, and seven crowns upon its head, drawing the third part of the stars of heaven after it."

And therefore he proceeds to preach against bribery. He thought it was the right time, "because the Legislature in New York is busy in investigating charges of bribery. The whole country woke up in holy horror at the charge that two thousand dollars had been offered to influence a vote in the Legislature, as if this was something new; as though in one State nine hundred and seventy-five thousand dollars had not been paid a legislator of the State Government by a railway company to get its charter and secure a dedication of public lands; as though three-quarters of the legislators of the United States had not, through bribery, gone into putrefaction whose stench reached heaven. After a few weeks' hunting the squirrel has stolen the hickory nut. Gentlemen in New York hunt out wrong by day and play poker and old sledge at night at Delavan House. It was like the country which had spent six millions of dollars in lawsuits about William Tweed going suddenly into hysterics when it found out that he had stolen a box of steel pens. California is submerged in the grip of a great monopoly; in Kansas United States senators had been involved in charges of bribery; in Connecticut an election to Congress was bought as men might buy a box of strawberries. Last year they were convicted of attempting bribery in Pennsylvania, but the Court of Pardons liberated them with the exception of two judges, who were told that they would be cut off from political preferment for their obstinacy. A Pennsylvania United States senator used to put a price on legislators just

as a Kentuckian puts a price on his horse." But it was
not legislators alone that Dr. Talmage attacked. He
declared that the railways, the common carriers of the
country, were tainted by a favouritism which was, in
fact, the result of bribery. One company made rebates
in its fares to some favoured corporation, as in the case
of a petroleum company, which was enabled to control
the price of that light all over the world in consequence
of a virtual monopoly that was given to it by arrange-
ment with the railway. In the same way merchandise
in grain, provisions, and cattle are placed in the hands
of a few firms. "How much," asks Dr. Talmage, "did it
cost the Elevated Railroad to keep the fare from dropping to five cents from ten cents? I have been told,"
said he, "three hundred thousand dollars," which is
60,000*l.* "Very seldom does a bill pass through any of
our Legislatures if there be no money in it. Sometimes the bribery is in bank bills, sometimes in railroad
passes, sometimes in political preferment, sometimes
by the monopolies given to the legislators, what are
called points, a corner, a flier, a cover, washing the
street, salting down, ten up! If you want to know
what these are, ask the bribed members at Albany and
Harrisburg." Then he goes on, with some truth, to
declare that the bribery begins far away behind all this;
that it is really with the money subscribed for election
expenses that the evil begins its course. "From the
big reservoirs of subscribed election expenses the little
rills roll down in ten thousand directions, and by the
time the great gubernatorial, congressional, and presi

dential elections are over, the land is drunk with bribery." Perhaps it is quite as well that it is from an American orator and from an American writer such statements and such indictments proceed, rather than from a stranger like myself; but it is very clear that the evil which De Tocqueville indicated long ago has spread rather than diminished, and there is reason to think that it will do so until the public conscience of a great people is aroused to a sense of the enormity of the mischief. But it lies far down towards the base of the national institutions, and any attempt to extirpate it will fail until the doctrines of the "Spoils to the Victors" be rejected from the political catechism, and the interests of party made the means and not the end of political life.

The letters which appeared in the *Morning Post,* written under the influence of the surprise and anger I felt at the extent and impunity of crimes of violence and the state of feeling, or want of it, respecting them in the West, were badly received in America, and were severely handled by a few papers, as I was informed; I expected that the mention of the subject would not prove agreeable, though I guarded myself most sedulously from a single offensive word —nay, went out of my way to palliate the offences against life and living, and to excuse the people who allowed them, whilst I most carefully drew the line—a broad one—between these border ruffians and the law-abiding, virtuous people of the settled States. I was not, however, prepared for misrepresenta-

tion. One would have thought that I accused the
kind hosts who had received us—our generous enter-
tainers in so many cities—the courteous, polished
gentlemen who accompanied us—of murder and robbery, and ascribed to them the brutal murders committed by Canty or the Kid. As I quoted chapter
and verse, and as the papers which vilified me could not
deny the statements, they wrote that I had been imposed upon by the vivid fancy—in other phrase, the
deliberate lying—of their brother editors in the West.
One organ had the effrontery to declare that the Duke
of Sutherland expressed his delight at the kind and
courteous treatment of the ruffians I denounced;
adding, "somebody lied—it was not the Duke." No.
It was not indeed! A friend sent me one of these,
and below an article in which it was said that I might
take my place " beside Basil Hall, Mrs. Trollope, and
Dickens for libelling the people of the United States,"
and that my stories were all inventions, there was a
pregnant commentary as follows:—Sunday, July
17th : Daring Train Robbery ; Bandits Boarding
Chicago, Rock Island, and Pacific Cars ; The Conductor and a Passenger Shot Dead, and the Safe in
the Express Car Robbed ; the Passengers Saved by a
Brakeman."

I hope it will not be imagined that I have any
desire to cast obloquy on the grand efforts, supremely
successful as they have been, to turn the prairie and
the desert to the uses of civilised man and of the
world, and to open up the Western Continent to

humanity and civilisation. I am too sensible of the courtesy, ready service, and hospitality everywhere accorded to the party of English travellers of which I was one, to write one word which I thought calculated to give pain or offence to any of our many friends or to any right-minded American. *Maculæ solis!* 'Tis a pity they are there! In a few years, perhaps, the memory that such things were will have passed away like the recollection of some evil dream. But public sentiment must make itself felt, and above all there must be some abatement of the maudlin sympathy, which is virtually on the side of crime, if it be active in averting punishment.

Crime in America, especially in the Eastern States, is very much the same as it is in other countries, but in the far West there is more recklessness in dealing with human life, which, in spite of the Howard Society and of humanitarians, I believe to be connected with the indulgence extended under State laws by American judges and juries to criminals who appear to be deserving of nothing but the strict and unmitigated application of the rope. " Property " is safe, for the citizens hunt down with extraordinary energy marauders whose object is simply plunder. Ordinary robbers and gangs of burglars are speedily and summarily suppressed. It is otherwise with those who assail life and limb. The desperadoes who infest the "saloons," as they are called, with which every western settlement is sure to be provided as soon as the shingle roofs are placed on the earliest upheaval

of deal planks which can be called a dwelling, have
far greater immunity and freedom than burglars or
robbers. Wherever the train stopped for water on
our journey in New Mexico, Western Colorado, or
Eastern California, a rectangular wooden box, with
a verandah, open doors, windows screened by a
muslin curtain, perhaps a flagstaff with the Stars and
Stripes flying, a large signboard, and some high-
sounding name — the "Grand Alliance," "Union
League," "El Dorado," "Harmonium," "Arcadia," or
the like—was visible, with the usual group of booted
and bearded miners, and their horses hitched up at the
door-posts in front; inside you would be certain to
find men of the same class at a bar, behind which,
known for miles around, the affable Charlie, Bill, or Bob
was dispensing drinks and mixing cocktails, slings, and
the other drinks, in which the badness of the spirit is
artfully disguised by a stimulant of a more active
character and more pronounced flavour, known as
"bitters," and kept in subjugation by the liberal use
of ice. For even in these burning regions ice is
stored up as the one thing needful. The rudest miner
is accustomed to it; iced drinks are consumed by
classes in America far below the social level of those
who never taste them in this country.

As the train was halting at Colorado Springs the
stewards engaged in an animated discussion respecting
a certain erection of poles and rafters just visible
in an adjacent field. "I tell you dat's it." "I say
tidn't." They were discussing the probability of the

scaffolding being the gallows whereon " Canty, the
Buena Vista murderer," was to be hanged the day
after. On April 29th, last year, Mr. Canty was
standing on the platform in front of Lake-house
with " Johnny the Ham," " Curly Frank," and " Off
Wheeler," when Thomas Perkins appeared in an alley
opposite, endeavouring " to induce ' Dutch Bill ' to go
with him to the office of Justice Casey, who had
deputised him for the purpose." Canty and his companions at once ran across and demanded his release.
Before Perkins could answer, Canty fired and missed
him. The second shot wounded Perkins in the arm ;
the latter drew his pistol, but before he could use it
Canty fired ; the ball shattered the constable's hand.
" For God's sake," he exclaimed, " is there no policeman to help me ? " He fell, and Canty, walking close
to his side, coolly sent a bullet through his body. He
was arrested, tried, and convicted. His counsel applied
to the Supreme Court for a *supersedeas*, but the court,
after solemn argument, refused the application. Then
they applied to the Governor of the State, but Mr.
Pitkin, though " a weak-kneed man," would neither
grant a reprieve nor a commutation to imprisonment
for life. There was, he said, no ground " to.set aside a
verdict of a competent jury and the district judge
reviewed and approved of by the Supreme Court." In
the very last hour a woman came forward, and the
Denver paper gave *verbatim et literatim* the text of the
document in which . . " with dew regard," she offered
Sheriff Spangler $50,000 (10,000*l.*) to save the life of

W. H. Canty, her cousin, whose real name was, she said, N. H. Salisbury. "I entreat you to have him spared till you have an interview with me." She added that "Jennings and his brother in Leadville would pay a still larger sum. You may have ample means for life," &c. A gentleman of the press, who came into our train at South Arkansas, was present at the execution. Just before the drop fell, Canty, who had expressed complete confidence in his ultimate liberation till the day before his execution, spoke for fifteen minutes, protesting his innocence. Then he exclaimed, "Good-bye, nothing can save me. I have faith in the Saviour and a hereafter." The trap was sprung, but to the horror of every one, the rope broke at the beam. The murderer's neck, however, was dislocated, and "a happy relief was experienced" when it was found he had died a painless death. As he was the nephew of an eminent stateman it was expected his friends would take action as to the disposal of his remains, which were put "in a neat casket at the sheriff's expense." In the journal there was a woodcut of the murderer. "Before his likeness could be taken holes were bored in the door and Canty was lashed to it, and then, when the door was set upright, the photographer watched a favourable opportunity when the head and eyes were quiet and secured the impression" from which the engraving was made. He was not so fortunate as Frank Gilbert, who was sentenced to be hanged the following day for a brutal murder, but respited, "in order that the proceedings may be reviewed by the highest judicial tribunal," by Governor Pitkin at the last moment, "till July 29," the day on which Rosencrantz is now sentenced to be hanged. The sheriff, Judge Ward, the clerk of the court, and the prosecuting attorney joined with others in petitions to the governor on the ground that the Supreme Court judges had refused a *supersedeas* in consequence of the defects and informalities of the record of the proceedings in the court below. Rosencrantz was respited, and the public, who had been expecting a double execution on the 18th of June, were disappointed, although they were allowed to slake their curiosity by the sight of the condemned men and by testing the ropes in the prison enclosure where the scaffold was ready. In the paper which gave the text of Governor Pitkin's reprieve there was a heading "Done Brown. Al. Huggins, marshal of Recene, turns out a bad man. He shoots and fatally wounds officer Brown of Kokomo." Phil. Foote, constable of Kokomo, formerly marshal of Robinson, and Al. Huggins, marshal of Recene, it seems had spent the night in visiting the saloons of Kokomo, and in the early morning began to fire their pistols and guns off in the street, and continued to do so until Andy Sutton, marshal of Kokomo, attempted to arrest them, but failed, "as he was quickly covered by two rifles." Mr. Brown, a police officer, asked Huggins to put up his pistol, and, to encourage him, proceeded to pocket his own revolver, when Huggins took deliberate aim with a 38-calibre Colt and shot Brown in the left breast, just above the heart. Huggins and Foote started for Recene. The marshal of Kokomo followed quickly in pursuit, with a large body of men. Huggins refused to surrender, whereupon the marshal shot him in the face. As there was a movement to lynch him, Al. Huggins was sent under strong guard to Leadville, but Foote escaped. "Brown was not dead by last accounts, but was not expected to live long." Then came a long account of another "Denver tragedy. Charles Stickney murders Mr. T. Campan and Mrs. H. O. Devereux in a boarding-house." Stickney was nephew of ex-Governor Clifford, of Rhode Island, served as lieutenant, 20th Regiment, in the war of 1861–4, graduated at Harvard, became principal of a school, married a lady whom he sent to London to study music, and tried mining whilst his wife was giving music lessons in Denver. There she met Mr. Campan, one of the best families in Detroit; Stickney shot him and killed a woman who was in the room at the same time. " Public opinion is in favour of Stickney, and he will probably be reprimanded." The evening of the day we reached Leadville, "Alderman Johnnie M'Combe, a leading candidate for lieutenant-governor and mayor, and last spring before the people for city treasurer," shot and wounded, probably fatally, a well-known actor named James M'Donald, because the latter had taken some children in M'Combe's buggy for a drive. It is not easy to determine how far Johnnie's chance of office may be affected by this ebullition, but the newspapers did not write of it with harshness; one gave it a comic character by the heading, "Ex-

Alderman M'Combe attempts to perforate Jemmy M'Donald's cranium." In my morning paper of the same date I find that "James Hogan was foully murdered by James M'Cue in the open streets of Erie this afternoon in a quarrel about a handkerchief;" that Dr. Flemings, a prominent citizen of Portland, Ashley County, Arkansas, had appeased a quarrel between a pedlar named Gillmore and a coloured man very effectually, for, "incensed by a remark made by the pedlar, the doctor drew a pistol and shot him dead;" that "a prominent business man of M'Leansboro' had made a sensation on the streets to-day by hunting up, pistol in hand, one of the gay Lotharios of Hamilton County;" that "Daniel Keller, deputy county clerk, was stabbed and killed in the street of Virginia City by Dennis Hennessy, a kerbstone broker;" that "a searching party under Captain Leper had overhauled Hamilton, Myers and Brown, the outlaws who shot Sheriff Davis and Collector Hatter at Poplar Bluff, Mo.; killed Hamilton, mortally wounded Myers, and made Brown a prisoner;" that "James Hurd shot Jeff Anderson at Alamosa, Col., and that it was feared the latter would not survive." An account of the death of "Curly Bill," a notorious desperado, leader of cowboys and murderer of Marshal White, who was killed at Caleyville, Arizona, by his comrade, Jem Wallace, followed. They had a quarrel (of course, in a saloon). After a few drinks "Curly Bill" said, "I guess I will kill you on general principles." Wallace stepped out of the saloon and imme-

diately opened fire, inflicting a mortal wound on his
foe. After a brief hearing Wallace was discharged,
and left for parts unknown. Then it was related
how "Thomas Clarey ('Tommy the Kid'), a Durango
outlaw, was killed by a comrade named Eskridge at
Annego while drunk." A fratricide and three trials for
murder were, duly recorded. Another paper gave an
account of South-West Colorado from the lips of a
recent visitor to San Juan County. "Are you going
back to San Juan? No, I think not; but it is a
glorious country. The men there are a little rough,
and kill each other on slight provocation; but a peace-
able man who does not swagger and blow is not mo-
lested. There is no law, and courts and constables are
unknown." He narrates how Aleck ——, acting as a
barkeeper, "a noble-hearted, jovial fellow, full of fun,
who looked you square in the eye, owns mines, said
to be worth a million," settled a difficulty; I am
inclined to think Mr. Charles Klunk rather drew on
the interviewing reporter of the *Globe Democrat*.
He was, he said, going to see a stockman who lived
about fifty miles from the house where he was
visiting. A farmer said to him "Come and take a
drink with me, and I'll show you the barkeeper who
killed the man you are going to see an hour ago."
The stockman had come into the saloon whilst Aleck
was in the back room, and began to abuse him. Aleck
heard him, opened on the man with a revolver, and
"shot him full of holes. Next day I asked him what
he was going to do about it, and he said he had been

tried and acquitted, which meant that some of the leading men had told him that he had done right. There was no trial about it. When a man kills another out there in a fight they don't inquire very strictly into the circumstances, but make up their minds that they can't bring the dead man to life by hanging the killer, so nothing is done about it. But when a man murders another to rob him, the vigilants turn out and have no mercy on him. They just fill his skin with lead and tumble him into a hole like a wolf. After all, though the bears are plentiful in the spring, you can kill a deer 100 yards from the house where you like, the streams are alive with trout, the vegetables and crops splendid." Mr. Charles Klunk's resolution not to go back to this Happy Valley seems founded on sound constitutional principles. What I wish to point out is the condition in which the Central Government and State Governments have permitted many districts of New Mexico, Colorado, and California to remain. It is plain that the peculiar conditions under which the sway of the United States has been extended over the regions of the Far West have rendered it very difficult to establish the machinery for protecting life and property and punishing crime; but I do not see that the statesmen at Washington or the legislators at the State capitals are very much concerned at the reign of terror which prevails on the borders, or that they seek to impress on their people any regard for the sacredness of life. In fact, human life is almost a drug in the market. And I write

fully sensible of the failures of our own and of all
European Governments to repress crime, to prevent
violence, and to ensure security to life and property.
I am aware that Ireland and Poland are to the fore,
and that wife-beating and " running kicks " illustrate
the brutality of Lancashire and other districts—that
London has its Alsatias, that every European capital
has foul recesses in which the only laws are those
of crime. All the world is busy preparing shoals of
emigrants for the United States. It is only, however,
when some savage outbreak affrighting the propriety
of a great city arouses indignation and fear that there
is a clamour for measures of repression. I do not
think there is in any óther part of the world, or
that there ever has been in any civilised country,
such shootings as have filled the land to which
I allude with bloodshed. It may be said with
truth that there never have been and that there are
not any similar conditions in the world. But the
absence of any great abiding movement for the cor-
rection and suppression of violence and lawlessness
cannot be so readily accounted for or excused. There
appears to be a sort of admiration for these border
ruffians among portions of the American Press and
public. Even a staid paper like the *Republican*, in
an article headed " South-East Missouri : the Reign of
Lawlessness about Ended," on the destruction of the
New Madrid gang, writes of one who was sent to the
penitentiary for thirty years " as a living monument
of a bold and brave lot of desperate men who had

started out to make money by robbing their fellow-men. This swift and stern justice speaks well for this portion of the States, which has had for a long time more than its full quota of these lawless characters. Myers and Brown will be hung on the 15th July, and their execution will be witnessed by thousands of South-East Missourians." The spectacle of the hanging will not do much good, if it be like the execution at Colorado Springs, which was advertised as a sort of picnic or pleasure excursion. One advertisement ran, "After the hanging to-morrow drink La Salle beer; it will cool your nerves." "Highway robbery here has about run its course, and the people are determined that law-lessness in those regions shall no longer go unwhipped of justice." Very good. But, why not sooner and long ago? "Rhodes was hung by Judge Lynch when captured at the killing of young Laforge in New Madrid;" but the gang killed the sheriff and wounded the deputy-sheriff and collector before the people arose in their majesty to squelch them. A criminal is in-vested with a notoriety which, next to popular estima-tion, is valued by some men, and it is noted with interest that "Gilbert" (one pitiless murderer) is a Catholic, and that "Rosengrants" (another homicide) "inclines towards the Episcopalians." A Leadville doctor visits one of them to ask for his body. "No, sirree, you can't have my body; I'll be hanged first!" And the public laugh at the lively sally, and admire the *sangfroid* of the wit! In fact, there is a *tendresse* for crime in this grim humour. A Texan who

would "fill the skin" of a stranger "with lead" for
aspersing Texas would no doubt heartily enjoy the
description of the early population of the Lone Star
State, which I quote from the Texas Press. "In the
early days of the Republic, and even after annexation,
many of the white men who came here had strong
sanitary reasons for a change of climate, having been
threatened with throat disease so sudden and dangerous
that the slightest delay in moving to a new and milder
climate would have been fatal, the subjects dying of
dislocation of the spinal vertebræ at the end of a few
minutes—and a rope. A great many left Arkansas,
Indiana, and other States in such a hurry that they
were obliged to borrow the horses on which they rode
to Texas. They mostly recovered on reaching Austin,
and many invalids began to feel better and consider
themselves out of danger as soon as they crossed the
Brancos River. Some who would not have lived twenty-
four hours longer had they not left their homes reached
a green old age in Western Texas, and were never again
in risk of the bronchial affection already referred to by
carefully avoiding the causes which led to their trouble.
Some at Austin recovered so far as to be able to run for
office, within a year, though defeated by a respectable
majority, owing to the atmosphere and the popularity
of the other candidate." The most extraordinary
fact connected with the indulgence which is extended to Western excesses is the severity with which
Northern and Eastern writers and publicists deal
with the recklessness of Southerners with regard to

life, as if it were a political question in some way
connected with slavery. In an article on " Coloni-
sation," in the July number of ' The International
Review,' there is an attempt to prove that the prevalence of homicide in the South as compared with the
North has impeded the flow of immigrants, although
slavery has disappeared, and the writer, quoting Mr.
Redfield's book on ' Homicide North and South,' says
the terrible "scourge of open murder, wholly irrespec-
tive of political causes more deadly than disease or
yellow fever, because each death is the result of a
heinous crime, seems to be calmly accepted by public
opinion as a part of the unchangeable conditions of
social life in the South. In Kentucky more men are
killed in six days than in eight years in Vermont. In
a village of Connecticut a death from homicide has
never occurred from its foundation, while in one grave-
yard in Owen County, Kentucky, the majority are
murdered men, and in another county forty-two persons
were killed and forty-three wounded in two years."
But in the very same number of the ' International '
there is an account of the doings of the " Vigilance
Committee " of San Francisco (where there were no
slaves and where there is immense wealth), which
might cause the author of the paper on " Coloni-
sation " to reflect a little on his theories. Surely in
Arizona, California, &c., where the foreign population
is 50 per cent. of the natives, immigration has not been
checked by the prevalence of homicide? It must not
be supposed that there is no " law " in the towns where

these crimes have been committed; in all the cases
referred to the coroner did his office and verdicts were
returned, and it will have been seen that "wretches
hang" in due course.   We had intended to visit the
State prison at Cañon City on our way to Pueblo from
Leadville, where we were promised an opportunity of
seeing "thirty murderers all in a row," but the delay
of the train on the road deprived us of the means of
verifying the statement, and I give it as it was made.
It would seem as if the criminal supply were super-
abundant, or that death on the gallows had no deter-
rent influence.   The chances of escape are, if not
numerous, at least considerable.   At Deming, Denver,
Leadville, Tucson, Tombstone, and other cities, the
vast mass of the inhabitants are law-abiding, peace-
able, honest, and honourable men, who feel as much
horror at the violence and bloodshed around them as
the most refined lady in any saloon of Boston, Paris, or
London, but they appear to endure these things in
the hope that the law will be enforced at last; now
and then they break into vigilance committees and
execute their own decrees, though the judges do not
fail to lay it down that they have been accessories to
murder.   The great civiliser and police agent is the
railroad.   It is affirmed that as the iron way is pushed
on the outlaws and the *personnel* of outlawry congre-
gate at the terminal town, but I suspect that there is
a fringe of the material left on the border as it runs.
As our party were at dinner in the palace-car one
evening the train pulled up at a station.   There was a

group of rough men on the platform, who stared in with all their eyes at the white tablecloth, set with bright glass and silver, and at the cheerful faces under the lamps. " How merry they are. I wonder if they know that this is Dodge City ? " exclaimed one of the crowd. I was told by an official that when they were making a railway in these parts the surveyors, &c., were much troubled by gangs of gamblers and robbers, who impeded the work and debauched the men, so after due warning they made a razzia on the gamblers, shot a lot of them, and the rest "vamosed." There was not very long ago an actual war in the Grand Cañon Valley between the Atchison, Topeka, and Santa Fé Railway and the Denver and Rio Grande Railway, in which there was an array of armed forces and fighting on both sides, and we saw with our own eyes the remains of the breastworks cast up in the Grand Cañon by the belligerents. The law came in at last. " One side got at the judge first and gave him $50,000. The other was quite ready to go beyond that, but the first was too quick, and the suit went against the company." I was talking to a lawyer about the length of time which is allowed by the judges to criminals sentenced to death as a detail of the execution of the law not in accordance with the general practice of civilised nations, when one of the company remarked, " They must do it, sir, to please the people. If we had Judas Iscariot in gaol to-morrow there would be thousands of petitions to commute his sentence, and thousands of dollars ready for an appeal

to the Supreme Court. Our people don't like prompt
sentence." Nevertheless, sentence and execution are
pretty swift when the desperadoes take the law into
their own hands, as we have seen. The revolver and
the " saloon " are the agents and the scene in most of
these murders, and whisky is too often the motive power.
In Kansas it is a criminal offence to sell any intoxicating
spirit, or to use it except on medical certificate. It is
said that the law cannot last, but it surely was a very
strong conviction of the evils which were endured by
the community that brought a State Legislature,
elected by the people, to enact that beer, wine, and
spirits should be absolutely and entirely banished from
its borders. Lately there was a prosecution by the
State attorney of a man for selling spirits. The case
was clearly proved. The judge charged the jury in
the strongest manner against the defendant. The jury
without retiring at once found a verdict of " not guilty."
" Boys," exclaimed the judge, putting his hand on the
foreman's shoulder, " Boys, I'm quite with you." The
Kansas case will be, I think, watched with great
interest by the rival parties in England, and it is
certainly worth investigation and attention, for, if all
I hear be true here, a Parliament elected by the people
either in advance or in the rear of their constituents
have passed a law which judges condemn, and juries
evade, and public opinion derides.

From a British, which may be an unintelligent, point
of view, there is a want of logical method in the treatment of the Great Rebellion question by Americans.

There is a general disposition to speak of the war between the Federal Government and the people of the Confederate States as an historical fact which has ceased to present burning controversies and terrible issues to the Republic. But, at the same time, these controversies are kept alive, and, for the defeated, are stirred up incessantly by anniversaries and celebrations, natural but, if it be the object of Americans, as many of them assure us it is, to let the memory of the past die out like that of a horrid dream, impolitic. The spirit which animated the Southern States is neither dead nor sleeping. But there are no end of G. A. P. and G. A. R. Associations flourishing their banners and waving their sheathed swords in and out of the newspapers, and it is almost more than Southern flesh and blood can bear at times to be reminded of the defeats they sustained, even if they be content to admit that the doctrine of the sovereignty of States was a delusion, and that the indivisibility of the Republic was a fundamental principle of the Constitution before it was conclusively established by force of arms.

North and South, our good cousins are fond of anniversaries and speechmakings. I wonder where they get their taste for them from ? Some few veterans dine together on anniversaries of old French war days, and there is a Balaclava Dinner in the Old Country; but, though we have a reasonably long list of fighting successes to commemorate, their anniversaries are mostly left to the almanacks. The other

day the Americans had a celebration of the Battle of
Cowpens, wherein the heroic Morgan gave the diabolical
Tarleton the deuce of a whipping. I wonder if it was
worth remembering? But it is better to remember
such things perhaps than Sherman's Raid or Wilderness
—or Chickahominy. There are bitternesses enough
remaining—the rivalries and jealousies of generals are
still active and these memories might be left to die
out.

The great war which so deeply moved the population
of the United States has left many traces in Soldiers'
Homes, and men deprived of legs or arms, or bearing
marks of indelible wounds, are to be met with wherever
there is any considerable gathering of people all over
the Union. The clerk at the bar of the hotel, to
whom we were talking a moment ago, was a captain in
a regiment of militia, and served with distinction,
having risen to the grade he occupies by conduct and
courage during the war; and if he is known among
his friends by the title of "Colonel," he deserves,
probably, the brevet conferred upon him by the
authority of the general public around him. The
conductor of the train on the Pennsylvania Railroad,
to whose attention we were so much indebted, was an
ex-officer of volunteers, was engaged at the first battle
of Bull Run, where he was wounded, and in several
other actions. And our good friend the Major, who
enabled us to pass many an hour listening to his
admirable rendering of negro minstrelsy, bore in his
body a proof of the dangers he had passed, in the shape

of a Confederate bullet, or it might have been (for I am
not quite sure now) a projectile of the Federal per-
suasion. And so on. Scarcely a day passed that we
did not meet someone who had been fighting on one
side or the other.

One great change has come over Americans since I
was last here, and, whether it was the ridicule to which
they were exposed or to a sense of their greatness as a
nation that it be due, it is to be commended. Except
by a professional interviewer, not one of the party was
asked, " What do you think, sir, of our country ? " !

The welcome which an Englishman who is entitled
to admission into good society receives all over the
States, in the best houses, and from the best men, is as
gracious and warm as ever. It seems as if a reaction
against the suspicion, jealousy, and harshness which
marred the political relations of the Republic and Great
Britain in times gone by, moved those who behave with
so much courtesy to Englishmen, and that they seem to
say, *sotto voce*, " Come and see how I forget the wrongs
done to the United States by the Ministers of George
III. and his successors ! Admit that I can be as
magnanimous as I am rich and cultivated ! I am of
your house, but I have transplanted all the good
qualities of your race to American soil, and grafted
them on the tree of liberty which towers aloft in all
the splendour of Transatlantic luxuriance above us."

CHAPTER IX.

THE RED MAN AND HIS DESTINY.

Captain Pratt—Carlisle Barracks—An Indian Bowman—The Indian Question—The Pupils' Gossip—The "School News"—Indian Visitors—The White Mother—The India Office—White and Red —Quo Quousque?—Indian Title Deeds—The Reservations—The Indian Agencies—Missionary Efforts—The Red Man and the Maori.

ON the 5th of May the party visited Carlisle Fort or Barracks, one of the ancient military establishments of the Republic, where in the old times, speaking in an American sense, a considerable force was usually concentrated to keep watch and ward over the western frontiers, now extended thousands of miles away to the Pacific. The Barrack, which is a large quadrangle capable of containing a couple of regiments, is appropriated by the Government to this great experiment, the systematic education of the Indians of both sexes, whose families send them to school for the purpose of learning English and useful arts, mechanical and other, which may be of advantage to their people. It was, perhaps, one of the most interesting of the many little excursions which the Duke of Sutherland and his friends made in the States, and as it was the only one of the schools which we had an opportunity of seeing I shall proceed to give a little account of what we witnessed. In the first place let me express the sense which every one of us entertained of the real

sterling qualities of Captain Pratt who is in charge of
the school, and of the devotion and solicitude for
their charges of those ladies employed in the training
establishment. It may be asked how casual visitors
could judge of these things? The discipline, order,
progress, and perfect method visible in every room, and
the intelligence and good understanding between the
teachers and the pupils which could be perceived
throughout the establishment, were adequate proofs, I
think, that the praise is well deserved. At the time
of our visit there were something under three hundred
pupils, of whom perhaps two hundred were boys, and
these were engaged in their class-rooms, each section
of Indians being arranged according to nationality, if
such a term can be used. But, indeed, the tribes of
Indians differed from each other in personal appearance
far more than do the races which inhabit the European continent. It is true they nearly all have straight
wire-like black hair and eyes set deeply and rather
obliquely in faces which are frequently of the Mongol
type. But there is great diversity in the shape of the
head, the angle of the jaw, the formation of the mouth
and nose, the colour (when not tainted or "improved"
by an admixture of European blood, whether Mexican
or American or other) being pretty uniform, a rich
bronze, with something of a copper hue, predominating
in the young people. The boys were dressed in a plain
neat uniform of greyish-blue, military tunics and
trousers, well shod and comfortably equipped in all
respects. The girls, amongst whom, perhaps, taste for

eccentric finery was not unobservable, wore dresses less
uniform in appearance, generally neat and always clean ;
but their foot gear was rather eccentric. The rooms,
spacious barrack-like apartments, well ventilated, were
appropriated to the classes according to age and progress, the boys being separated from the girls. The
walls were hung with maps and furnished with educational coloured prints, and boards for arithmetical
exercises were in each apartment. The desks and stools
were such as would be seen in an ordinary school, and
if one had not looked at the faces of the pupils and
been struck by some of the strange characters on the
walls he would have thought himself in the middle
of some ordinary school ; save, perhaps, that his ear
would have missed the curious humming noise which
marks the industry of idleness or of legitimate work
in similar establishments in Europe. But here were
all these young savages, poring over their books or
boring with their pens, looking up at the visitors
scarcely with curiosity and applying themselves again
to their work, or answering questions put to them with
the composure which must be a portion of the Red
Man's nature.

I cannot recollect how many tribes there were represented at the Carlisle school ; but I was struck by
the race-distinctions which could be observed when
Captain Pratt, standing on a raised platform, called
out the names of each tribe. The little batches, in
some instances only one or two, stood up briskly and
looked somewhat proudly about, as much as to say,

" We are Sioux (or Apaches, or Ponchas, or Creeks), not like these other fellows." And the young ladies were, if one might judge from their expression, quite as proud of their own people as the boys. But the names these poor children receive are ludicrous. Not content with calling them by English names, or American, singularly misapplied, very often, as a name may be, their own Indian nomenclature is translated into English, so that we heard reading and reciting beside " Luke Phillips " and "Almarine McKillip " (a Scotch Creek) "Maggie Stands-looking " and " Reuben Quick-bear." There was something of sarcasm, I think, in the address of a Creek boy to the visitors. He said : " The Indian boys had come here to learn something about the use of the bow and hunting. Their people believed that if boys grew up to manhood without learning they would be of no use ; therefore they had sent the boys here to get education." Then, after some moral if trite reflections, the lad said : "You must understand that nearly everything that was made was made both for the present and the future. This bar-racks was not built for Indians, as I do not think the men who built it ever thought that it would be an Indian school; but things were made to do good both in the present and in the future." And then quoth he, looking at his white friends straight in the face : " The education which we are getting here is not like our own land, but it is something that cannot be stolen nor bought from us." And the white man did not turn red at the words ! I do not pretend to judge

of the actual progress made in learning, but the very
intelligent self-possessed teachers reported uniformly
that they were satisfied. The most useful education,
perhaps, which these Indians receive is in practical
mechanics, and a visit to the workshops attached to
the barracks was amply repaid by the sight of these
industrious young fellows hammering and leathering
away in the various departments. They have actually
completed waggons of a most satisfactory construction,
complete in all their parts, so much so that orders
have been received for as many as can be supplied for
the use of Agencies. They make and repair their own
shoes. They have sent out a hundred and twenty
double sets of harness. They make coffee-boilers,
cups, pans, pails, and all the articles known to the
tin-smith; and the girls are taught to hem and sew
and knit in the English fashion; but it must have
been not many a long year before the white man
landed, when the ancestors of these Indian maidens
exercised the same mystery with fine sinew and skin
in the wonderful work of which specimens are handed
down to us to-day. On one point alone, perhaps,
there was something to regret; the health of the
children was not all that could be desired. Well
clad, regularly fed, I presume on wholesome food,
cleanly lodged in well-ventilated rooms, these wild
children of the plains scarcely came up to the expectations one would form of them in the matter of chest-
measurement; and although many were remarkable
for fine physical development, Captain Pratt confessed

that their sanitary condition was not everything that could be desired, and that losses from consumption and other causes were rather serious. But they have plenty of out-door exercise. They have games in which they rejoice. They drill and march to the sound of their own band, a very good brass band of eight performers, each of a different tribe, who played "Hail Columbia!" and the "Star-Spangled Banner," and the like, with energy and zest; nay, with harmonious concurrence. When we went out into the large open square, there appeared before us a wonderful being in feathers, waving plumes, wampum and all the leathern panoply and peltry adornments of an Indian, painted, and armed with bow and arrow, probably such an one as Captain John Smith may have seen as he went exploring the woods of Virginia on his way to the sacrifice from which he was saved by Pocahontas. A target was erected at a distance of a hundred yards or so, and had I been in the centre of it, I should have been perfectly safe from the arrows which the Indian warrior discharged at it. But we were told that with a good bow a strong-armed Indian will drive an arrow right through a buffalo, and in that case I would suppose that the buffalo was very near to him indeed.

Of course it is but natural to find very varying degrees of intelligence amongst the pupils, and the rate of progress was by no means uniform, but a committee of examination which recently visited the school declared that the manifestations of advancement in the rudiments of English education were to them simply surprising. It was with admiration bordering on amazement they observed the facility and accuracy with which the children passed through the various exercises, in reading, geography, arithmetic, and writing, of the schoolroom; the accurate training and the amount of knowledge displayed were, they reported, the fullest proof not only of skilful teaching, but of great aptitude and diligence on the part of the children. Considering the brief period during which the school had been in operation, and the fact that the children entered it in a wholly untutored condition, the evidence was conclusive of the capability of culture. They go on to say: " We are fully persuaded that improvement equal to that which we have witnessed in the case of these children of the plains, if made in equal time by American children, would be regarded as quite unusual. And when the difficulty of communication consequent upon the diversities of language is taken into account we can but feel that the results of which we have been the witnesses to-day justify our judgment of them as amazing."

One of the most interesting features connected with the attempts to educate the Indians at Carlisle is the ' School News,' a little publication which, as I understand, is conducted by Indian pupils taught in the establishment, edited by Samuel Townsend, a Pawnee Indian boy. It is published once a month, and costs

25 cents or 1s. per year. It takes as its motto the lines:

> " A pebble cast into the sea is felt from shore to shore,
> A thought from the mind set free will echo on for ever more."

Perhaps neither the metre nor the actual statement commend themselves to acceptance, but the matter of the little journal is full of interest. In the first place the names of the contributors afford full matter for meditation. Perhaps it is one of the steps which must be taken to civilise these poor Indians that their names should undergo a strange and, to me, unmeaning metamorphose. There seems no reason whatever why the Indian names should not be retained, or if there is any reason for changing them, at least there might be some discrimination and good taste exercised in the adoption of English Christian names.

The first number of the 'School News,' which I have before me, contains as an article: "What Michael Burns, an Apache boy, thinks on the Indian Question." He says, "I cannot help myself, having much feeling for my people, what has been said about them, and the efforts making to give us the same privileges as the people of the United States. And it is said how we have been treated by the bad white man, for the last ten or fifteen years, decreasing our number. But that kind for treatment for my nation will soon stop." The poor boy goes on to say: "There is no doubt that we are in fault. We had the opinion that we

could not get beaten by any other nation. Now we
know for ourselves that we will have to change. . . .
But how does the white man know which way
is the best to do. Was he born that way? No!
Education gives him the light of knowledge." Then
a boy named Marcus Poko writes to his father: "I
want you to try hard and leave the Comanche way,
and to find the white man's way." In the leading
article, written, I presume, by Samuel Townsend, it is
said: "Indian ways will never be good any more, it
is all passed, gone away, and the other way is coming
up to take the place. We shall all be glad when we
all get into the civilised way of living, then the
Indians will not make so much trouble for the
American people. Some people say 'let the Indians
get out of the way. There is no use in trying to
advance them, kill them all they are like the wild
animals deaf and dumb, they never will learn anything. We have already paid so much money for
them they have never become civilised yet.' But all
good people say, 'Oh, yes, give them an education and
plenty of opportunities, and send more teachers among
them so they may come up beside us and live as
brothers and live in peace.'" There is a little paragraph
as to language. "There are a great many words in
the English," says the writer, "that the Indians have
no word for, so the white people who make the Indian
books have to make new Indian words. So the Indians
have to learn the new Indian words. Now we don't
know much about it, but we believe the Indians can

all learn to speak the same as the whites." Then there is a column about the school news : "Lizzie McRae, a Creek girl, made a very good corn bread the other day. We had some of it. It was right good I tell you." "Robert American Horse is a steady boy. He works in the blacksmith shop very well, and Mr. Harris never has to tell him but once how to do something." " One of the teachers had artificial violets on her belt. A Gros Ventre boy saw them, but did not know what they were, so he got up from his desk and went close to the teacher. He looked at it and then smelt it. When he smelt it he said, 'Pooh ! rags !' " " Boys, some time ago Captain Pratt gave us advice about throwing stones at birds. Some of the boys who understand most English did not listen. We want the birds to come and stay with us and sing for us, too. Let us remember about this, and not let Captain Pratt have to say it again." "Last Sunday some of the large girls had a prayer-meeting in the yard at the back of the girls' quarters. Nobody told them to do it, but they thought it would be a good thing." There is a long letter from Lizzie Walton, a Pawnee girl of thirteen years old, describing a trip to Philadelphia, and I believe there are very few girls of thirteen years of age in any school who could write more amusingly or better. The account of a magic lantern by Ada Bent, a Cheyenne girl, closes the number.

Letters from the children who are sent out to the farmers are published in this little periodical, and give a very pleasing picture of the lives and aptitudes of these Indians. Virginia, of Kiowar, writes from a farm, asking one of the teachers to pardon her for not having done so before; but "I have not much time," she says, "I am very busy set the table and wash dishes make my bed and make pies and cakes and try to make bread too, and the other things beside. . . . Sometime I make fire and bring in wood. Mrs. Borton is very kind lady she has two children one girl and boy. I love these little children very much." "My dear Miss H——, I am not bad a girl I help now a great deal. I pray for you almost every night, also when I wake up in the morning. I like to pray very much because I make myself good." And so on in a pleasant little gossiping way, frequently in very difficult language. There is an article in the 'School News' of July upon the shooting of President Garfield: "The man who shot him," says the writer, "we suppose, thought he would please some of the people in the United States. He thought he was very smart. If President were to die how would every white man, black man and the Indian feel? It was not in war when the President was shot, for our country don't have war any more, but in peace. . . . We all feel sorry because the President is suffering. We hope he will soon recover." It is stated that about a hundred boys and girls have gone out to work on the farms, and there are some trite remarks about the advantages of hard work as opposed to the disadvantages of laziness. "The farmers up country say the Indian boys can bind wheat first-rate." "Nelly Cook, Sioux, made 36 sheets in one day last week. Nellie Cary, Apache, made 32, and Ella Moore, Creek, made 30. Boys, do you think those girls are lazy?" The 'School News' has a reporter, it would appear, for the paper says that "Our reporter took a walk round in the shops to see what the boys were doing. In all the shops every boy was busy. In the carpenter shop there were Jock (Arapahoe), Ralph (Sioux), Elwood (Iowa), and Joe Gun (Ponca) sawing out window and door frames. Oscar (Cheyenne) and Michael Burns (Apache) were busy carving balcony posts; and Lester (Arapahoe) was outside chiselling a beam. These things are all for our new hospital. . . . Jesse (Arapahoe) and Little Elk (Cheyenne) were busy in the gymnasium. The waggons which Robert American Horse has finished painting are to be sent to Oregon and Washington Territories." It is sometimes difficult to make out the meaning of the little prattle which these small people commit to the uncertain medium of the English tongue; but, on the whole, it is a most interesting and curious study. In one respect these children of the forest possess that which civilisation seems rather to dwarf amongst men of the highest culture and imagination—a certain stately eloquence and nobility of expression, in which natural images abound, and allegory and metaphor consort together in excellent and tasteful union. In a paper called 'Eadle Keatah Toh,' which seems to have been the precursor of the 'School News,' there is an inter-

esting report from the Committee on Indian Affairs to
the House of Representatives, submitted by Mr. Pound.
The motto of the paper is "God helps those who help
themselves"; but surely it might be better put that God
will help those who seek to do good to the unfortunate
Indians, who in contact with civilisation are rendered
utterly helpless, and who in their attempts to help themselves according to the manner of the race must meet with
nothing but extinction. From time to time there are
notices of deaths. One would like to know who wrote
the account of the "death of John Renville, son of
Gabriel Renville, Chief of the Sisseton Sioux." After
noticing the circumstances under which he contracted
his fatal illness—fever, produced by drinking water
at a spring on a hot day on a march to the camp in
Perry County, the writer says:—"'Death loves a
shining mark,' the poet sang long ago; and in the
passing away of John Renville from our school we
sadly say, how truthfully the poet sang. . . . .
Through all the days of his sickness his large sorrow-
ful eyes had a far-away wondering look, no pain
marred the beauty of his brow, and his voice as he
addressed his sister, who tenderly watched over him,
was like the trumpet warbling of some mournful bird.'
Our hearts follow the father in deep sympathy as he
bears back the body of his beautiful boy to the land
of the Dakotas for burial."

The Indian chiefs have a right, which they often
exercise, of visiting these schools as a Board; and
there is an account in the Carlisle paper of the visit

of Spotted Tail, Iron Wing, White Thunder, Black
Crow, and Louis Robideau from the Rosebud Agency;
Red Cloud, American Horse, Red Dog, Red Shirt,
Little Wound, and Two Strike from the Pine Ridge
Agency; Like the Bear and Medicine Bull from
the Lower Brule Agency; Son of the Star, Poor
Wolf, Peter Beauchamp, and John Smith from
Fort Berthold; Two Bears, John Big Head, Grass,
Thunder Hawk, and Louis Primeau from Standing Rock; Charger and Bull Eagle from Cheyenne
River; Brother to All and James Broadhead from
Crow Creek; Strike the Ree and Jumping Thunder
from Yankton; Robert Hakewashte and Eli Abraham
from Santee Agency; Mr. Tackett and his wife
and daughter; a daughter of Spotted Tail, and
others. The meeting of the children with their
parents is described as being most touching; and
sometimes the pupils were not recognised, so greatly
had they altered. As the chiefs seemed unwilling to
speak when called upon to do so, there was silence for
a time till a little girl, who had been about a year and
a half at the school, expressed her desire to speak in so
earnest a way that General Marshall permitted her to
do so; and so, speaking in her own dialect, her words were
translated into English and into Sioux. She declared
that she liked the white man's ways and the white man's
language. Indian words, she said, were down on the
ground, but the white man's language was in his head.
The chiefs, who listened attentively, seemed to understand this curious figure of speech, and nodded their

approval. And then she enlarged upon the advantage of what she learned, and implored the chiefs to send their children to the school, where she says she is going to try to be God's daughter. Her words seemed to kindle the fire within the chieftains' breasts, for Like the Bear, a Sioux, and father of one of the boys at Hampton School, came forward and addressed the meeting. "There is no greater power in the world," said he, " than the Great Spirit, and we must listen to Him and do what He wants us to do. When the men who were sent out by the Great Father the President asked for my children I gave them up. I see you are making brains for my children, and you are making eyes for them so that they can see. That is what I thank the Great Spirit for, and it is that which will make me strong." Then Robert Hakewashte, a chief from the Santee Agency, spoke, and said that he wanted schools like that which he saw here on his own reservation, and Spotted Tail wished for the same thing. "Since I have learned the words of God," he says, "it makes no difference to me what is the colour of a man's skin; if he walks like a man it is the same. I do not believe God likes the white colour only. God likes red and white, for He made them all." And then the flood of eloquence was loosened, and an old chief of the Sioux, nearly blind, verging on ninety years of age, who had come to see his grandson, said: "I grew up a red man, and the things I see here I never had a chance to see before. I have heard about the white man's church and his religion, and I have heard about the holy house. I have looked into them, and I am very much pleased. But there is only one Great Spirit we all can worship, and the red men all over the country are hearing about it. You are teaching the children to worship the Great Spirit. That is a great thing, and I like it. But you have here two sons of one father. One is sick. I want you to keep the other." And so he carried him away.

The condition of the Red Man who is allowed to exist under the banner of the Republic is a subject which has attracted the attention of the best and wisest men in the United States. The treatment of the Indians is a question of future policy. It is one which must exercise a very deep and abiding influence on the whole history of an ancient and interesting people. But it is exceedingly difficult to put in a short compass its most salient points before those who are unacquainted with the nature of the problems to be solved. Comparisons are odious, above all places, in America, when they are not to the advantage of the Great Republic, and I shall not draw any between the state of the Indian tribes in Canada and in the States. But it may be fairly admitted that the Indian Question in Canada is divested of many of the difficulties which surround it south of the lakes. The people of Canada have far more land than they know what to do with. They are a sparse population. They are not impelled to fierce adventures by mining "booms," and they are altogether less progressive than their American brethren. Shall we say that they are more charitable, more humane, less greedy of other men's goods? I do not say so. But at all events it is perfectly true that the Red Man, although he is dying out under the influence of whiskey and other influences which need not be particularised, in his native land, lives in comparative peace and comfort under the British flag in Canada. He is content with the White Mother. He pursues the occupations dear to his race as a hunter and as a fisherman. He is a dealer in peltries, and in such small barter as his needs require. He is the companion of sportsmen, and he delights, free as mountain air, to hunt on the hillside and in the prairie in winter over the vast ranges of snowy fields which in the few short months of spring and summer teem with flowers, and the frosty lakes which yield fish to his spear and net. There are few or no railways through his reservations to vex his repose, no great trains of miners with pick and rifle to drive away the moose and the buffalo, and hand the native hunter over to starvation. The Indian gives to the white man all he needs, and aids him in obtaining from the wide stretch of land over which he roams all the wealth that it can afford. Practically one part of the Dominion is handed over to the Red Man and to the half-breeds, for there is an Indian frontier which as yet has not been much encroached upon by any large migration of whites. As far as I know, conflicts north of the Saint Lawrence between Indians and whites are unknown, or have not been heard of for very many years. South of the great lakes, in the wonderful land over which is displayed the

banner of the stars and stripes, the fate of the Indian
is very different. In the words of Mr. Carl Schurz,
himself an expert in the question, "the history of the
relations of the United States with the Red Man
presents in great part a record of broken treaties, of
unjust wars and of cruel spoliation." That is a sweep-
ing statement, which it would be just as well for an
Englishman not to make, but coming from the mouth
of an American citizen and of a United States Minister
with plenty of evidence to back it, there can be no
harm in recording my conviction of its truth. It is
but another indictment against a defect in the form of
government which Americans exalt as the most perfect
of human institutions, that the central government
made treaties in good faith with the Indian tribes, but
was unable to enforce their obligations or to maintain
their integrity. There is, as all well-informed people
know—well informed, at least, in reference to American
affairs—a commissioner who makes an annual report
to the Secretary of the Interior respecting the Indian
tribes in the various locations over the Union and
the Territories. The last of these reports which I
have seen is that of the Acting Commissioner Mr.
Marble, addressed to the Department of the Interior
from the office of Indian Affairs at Washington in the
November of last year. The volume contains the
reports of the agents in the Indian Territory; of the
schools for Indian children established in pursuance of
a wise and humane policy, and detailed statistics in
relation to the Indian settlements and reservations, the

latter indeed forming by far the largest portion of the volume of 400 pages. Before I call attention to the condition of the Indians, and the efforts made to save them from extinction or from a degradation worse than annihilation, I should like to direct the attention of those who are interested in the subject to the view which is beginning to find favour, I believe, among the most experienced men in the States, that the system of "Reservations" is founded on a mistake the magnitude of which is demonstrated every day, and that the only means of saving the Indians from extinction is their gradual absorption as educated communities in the agricultural life of the nation, keeping them far as may be from the white man, but making no other distinction between them and the other citizens of the United States than such as must be found in the nature of the Indian race and their degree of culture and civilisation — treating them, in fact, as communities of Mennonites, Mormons, or Norwegians, or other nationalities would be treated in the United States. When the Reservations were first established it was considered impossible that the migration of the whites would extend to the remote regions of the west to which the unfortunate survivors of the people with whose virtues and vices Cooper and other novelists have made us familiar were gradually and often remorselessly driven. It is a plea which will be urged in bar of judgment that the doctrine of States Rights prevented the interference of the United States Government on behalf of the Indian tribes who were often ruthlessly destroyed. But it will scarcely be a plea, I think, which humanity in full court would recognise as valid. *Homo homini lupus*. But to the Red Man as to the Black in many cases the White Man is worse than any wolf; far more bloodthirsty and rapacious than any tiger—a Cain of Cains. It was our own kith and kin who, landing on the shores of the North American continent, encroaching by degrees upon the tribes and at last encountering their hostility, spread their sway literally by fire and sword, and rooted out the Red Man wherever they found him established on land or by sea which they coveted. We, whose country-men have worked out the same policy on the Australian continent and Van Diemen's Land, and who can only be restrained from its pursuit in New Zealand by the strong arm of the Home Government, can scarcely afford to take up stones to fling at our American brethren; and it is not with any purpose of indictment or accusation that I proceed to make a few remarks on the relations of the United States Government with the Red Man, and the efforts which they have been making to compensate the Indians in some measure for the injustice and persecution dealt out for many a generation.

As I looked at the men gathered at some of the railroad stations in the western desert and thought of the Red Men whose fate it is to meet such repre-sentatives of civilisation and Christianity, I could not but be filled with pity for the unfortunates and with wonder at " the dispensation " under which they live.

The faces are fine and bold enough, bearded to the cheek or shaved in the American fashion, with bold staring eyes, which "look square" in your own, with a general expression "Do you want a fight?" in them —the heads to which they belong are generally set on muscular bodies. If a gang of these men think fit to go on to an Indian reservation—the very name is too often a bitter mockery—who is to stop them? If the Indians try to do so and one of the white intruders is killed the country-side rings with cries of "vengeance for the massacre of our brethren," and all the papers are filled with accounts of "Another Indian Outbreak."

"The average frontier-man in the States looks," as Mr. Schurz says, "upon the Indian merely as a nuisance in his way. There are many whom it would be difficult to convince that it is a crime to kill an Indian." I will go further and say that there are many, I believe, who would take great pleasure in killing an Indian whenever they could; or as one gentleman observed to me, and I believe in his relations with white men no more just or honourable man or more humane could be found, "I would sooner kill an Indian than I would a skunk." When I was in the West, there was a cry raised that the Utes were about to wage war, and appeals appeared in the local papers for a military force to march against them. Their leaders were accused of arrogance and of insolence, and of murderous designs, and the general remark one heard was, "The Utes must go." I inquired a little into the matter when I got back, and I found that the Utes were strictly and absolutely, in their own right, standing upon the titles, which they had derived from the United States Government, to the lands from which they were required to move. These lands were wanted. Other lands were pointed out to them, to which they objected, and then they were informed that they would be moved by force, and preparations were made to levy war against these unfortunates, if they resisted deportation from the territory which had been assigned to them by the Great Father. Had they been Irish landlords, they could not have been treated worse; but in the West not one word was raised in favour of their claims.

The first point which has to be considered is, that the Indian is obnoxious to the very class of men with whom he is by the necessity of things most closely brought in contact. The railway has been the great persecutor of Red Men. It has driven away the game, it has carried in proximity to their reservations all the enterprise charged with whiskey, revolver, rifle, and greed, which can be furnished by the offscourings of the world. In the Far West the miners in advance throng into the valleys, and break the silence of the mountain-ranges by the sound of their picks, the cattle-raisers spread out over the plains, the ploughman settles down on the fertile land. " What," asks the American philanthropist, and his question is echoed all over the world by humane and good men, " what is to become of the Indian ? " The hunting-grounds are gradually being pushed farther west and north until they are bounded by the sea, and by the eternal snow. And if by any chance it should be found that there is gold or lead, silver or iron, or copper, or coal in any abundance, even under these unpromising conditions it will be sought. The buffalo is disappearing fast, faster than the Indian himself. Deer are becoming scarcer every year. What is to be left for the Red Man? Pastoral life and agriculture, say the philanthropists. The substitution, however, is not so easy. The weakness of the United States Government is the main cause why the policy of reservations has failed. Let us take the account of it by a United States Minister. "The Government," says Mr. Schurz, "has tried to protect the Indians in good faith against encroachments, and has failed. It has yielded to the pressure exercised upon it by people in immediate contact with the Indians. When a collision between Indians and whites once occurred, no matter who was responsible for it, our military forces were always found on the side of the white against the savage. How was Government to proclaim that white men should for ever be excluded from the millions of acres covered by Indian reservations, and that the national power would be exerted to do so?" Such an idea the American Minister thinks would be utterly preposterous. The rough and ready frontier-man would pick quarrels with the Indians; the speculators would urge him on. Government could not prevent collisions; the conflict once brought on, Government, in spite of its good intentions and sense of justice, would find itself employing its forces to hunt down the Indian. The old story would be repeated, as it will be wherever, says Mr. Schurz, there is a large and valuable Indian Reservation surrounded by white settlements, "and unjust, disgraceful as it is, that is an inevitable result." Such being the case then, the United States Government being powerless to see that right shall be done, and it being at once a human and a Christian duty to avert, if possible, the extinction of the original possessors of this grand continent, let us see what can be done to carry out the object. Fit the Indians, it is said, for the habits and occupations of civilised life ; give them individual possession of land as property, a fee-simple title to the fields they cultivate, guarded by an absolute prohibition of sale—because it has been found that whenever the Indians are exposed to the temptation of artful traders, they will be cajoled out of the titles they have to their land—and you will save the remnants from utter destruction. I hope it will be so. I could not but feel a glow of enthusiasm when I heard the Attorney-General, Mr. MacVeagh, at Washington, speaking incidentally one day about some railway matter, declare that he would not sanction the making of a line of railway through Indian Territory until he was satisfied that the Indians actually understood the conditions which had been offered to them by the company. "I will," said Mr. MacVeagh, "send down government agents there to ascertain that the Indians thoroughly understand what they are doing, and that it is of their own free will and consent that the railway passes through their territory in exchange for the money and goods they receive for the concession." Excellent and just minister! But, alas! I believe that ere I left the United States the whole thing was done; the railway company had declared that they would, whether or no, make their line, and if an Indian touched a hair of the head of any white man, the United States Government would not be able to avert the Divine wrath of every white man on the border from the whole of the tribe. Well may Mr. Schurz say that the thought of exterminating a race once the only occupants of the soil, where so many millions of our own people have flourished, must be revolting to every American who is not devoid of all sentiments of justice and humanity. Extermination or civilisation is the alternative offered to the Indian. Now let us see how it is proposed to civilise them. According to the returns in the Report for 1880, the number of Indians in the United States, exclusive of those in Alaska, is 256,127. Of these, 138,642 are described as wearing citizen's dress. It will be observed that there is no estimate given of the Indians who do not wear citizen's dress under this head. Citizens must be sometimes very badly dressed indeed if the Indians I saw at various stations along the line to San Francisco in shocking bad hats and tattered clothes were to be included amongst those who figured under this description in the report of the Commissioner. About 17,000 houses are reported as occupied. There are 224 schools, attended by 6000 scholars for a month or more during the year, scattered over the continent. About 34,550 Indians could read. There were 154 church buildings and 74 missionaries. The number of children of school age was 34,541; but this was an under estimate. Of these there was only school accommodation for 9972. · The total amount expended for education during the year by the United States Government was $249,299; by the State of New York, $15,863; by the State of Pennsylvania, $325; by other States, nothing; by religious societies, $46,933; by tribal funds, $7481. 22,048 Indian families were engaged in cultivating farms or small patches of ground; 33,125 male Indians were labouring in civilised pursuits; and 358 Indian apprentices had been pursuing trades during the year. This census and these statistics are stated to be imperfect, and it would require a close examination of the returns to enable an inquirer to form any idea as to the progress made in the direction which we are told is the alternative of destruction.

The Reservations of the various Indian tribes are scattered irregularly over the United States; from Michigan, Wisconsin, and Minnesota on the north and north-west, away to the Territories on the other side of the Rocky Mountains, down to New Mexico and Arizona, there being none in the southern states bordering the Atlantic. But there are Red Men of different tribes located, as the Americans would say, in the States to the east, such as New York. The Reservations are of irregular size and extent. Isabella, in the State of Maine,

reserved for 848 Indians, lies to the east of 86° longi-
tude, and south of 44° latitude. There is a considerable group of Reservations on the western shore of
Lake Michigan in Wisconsin, and in Minnesota. But
the proper Indian territory lies west of Arkansas,
with the Red River on the south, New Mexico on
the west, and Kansas on the north; and in it are
concentrated the Cherokees, Choctaws, Chicasaws,
Comanches, Cheeynnes, and several other tribes. The
Navajo Reservation in New Mexico and Arizona ranks
perhaps next in size, extending northwards into
Colorado, where the Utes have got a large tract of
land assigned to them upon what appears now to
be very doubtful or vanishing tenure. These, and
numerous reservations, which it would be tedious to
enumerate, are under the charge of agents appointed
by the Government at Washington, as to whose
functions and personal character and attainments one
hears very surprising and contradictory reports. But
I confess, from a perusal of the documents which they
have furnished to the head of the Department, and
which are published in the Annual Report, there
seems to me no just ground for imputing to these
gentlemen want of zeal, knowledge, interest, or
intelligence. Those who detest the whole work of
saving the Red Man are very apt to impute to the
Indian agents not only corrupt practices in relation to
the sale of government stores and supplies destined
for the use of those under their charge, but illicit
traffic in spirits, which is ruinous to the Red Man,

and even some participation in the acts of violence which have frequently led to Indian troubles. It all depends upon the manner in which your informant in the States regards the Indian Question whether the agents are described as scoundrels whom no man could trust, or as gentlemen of high propriety and general excellence.

The necessities which have been imposed by advancing civilisation of providing Indians with food entail a heavy outlay upon the United States Government, which is much begrudged by large sections of members of Congress, although they do not see their way clearly to withhold supplies of food from the unfortunate people whose hunting-grounds have been occupied, and who have not yet learned the arts of agriculture, so as to be able to supply themselves with food. The transportation of stores, the cost of beef, corn, coffee, bread, tobacco, tea ; in fact, all kinds of food, woollen goods, clothing, boots, hats, groceries, waggons, tools, hardware, and medical supplies,—all these duly figure in the estimates of the Indian Commissioner to a very considerable amount, and the returns as yet do not present any large reduction on the annual charge ; although nearly all the agents speak in terms of great hopefulness of the extraordinary advance which has been made in their agencies in the cultivation of the soil.

One remarkable division of the agencies has reference to their appropriation to religious denominations. An Indian might well be puzzled as to his form of belief if he were passed through the various agencies, attending at each a religious service or two, and listening to the teaching of the various divines attached to them. The Society of Friends have control of the belief and religious teaching of the Sante and Nemaja Indians in Nebraska, and of the Pawnees in the Indian Territory; to the Methodists are assigned three tribes in California, three tribes in Washington Territory, two in Oregon, three in Montana, two in Idaho, and one in Michigan. The Nevada Cherokees, Creeks, Choctaws, Chicasaws, and Seminoles are handed over to the Baptists. The Presbyterians have charge of the Nezpercès in Idaho, Umtas in Utah; the Apaches, Pueblos, and two other tribes in New Mexico. The Congregational Church exercises its religious offices among the tribes in Wisconsin, among two tribes in Dacotah, and one in Washington Territory. The Reformed Church has its work cut out for it in Arizona amongst four tribes. The Protestant Episcopal Church exercises its jurisdiction over one tribe in Minnesota, six tribes in Dacotah, one in Indian Territory, and one in Wyoming. The Unitarians have apparently only one tribe in teaching, the Los Pinos in Colorado. The United Presbyterians have one tribe in Oregon; the Christian Union has another in Oregon; the Evangelical Lutheran has charge of the Southern Utes in Colorado; and lastly, the Roman Catholic Church has two tribes in Washington Territory, two in Oregon, one in Montana, and two in Dacotah. As a general rule, the reports of the missionaries themselves are more sanguine, as they are wont to be, than are those of disinterested, perhaps unprejudiced, observers of their work. But, as is natural, the actual progress made depends very much, not only upon the nature of the tribe among whom the work is carried on, but on the character of the missionary, and on his ability and energy. In some instances, I see the condition of a tribe is reported as being lamentable, from a religious point of view, whilst in a neighbouring reservation, it is stated that great progress has been made in the establishment of religious teaching and ideas. The Rosebud Agency is said to prosper in the hands of one reverend gentlemen; the fathers of St. Ignatius are described as doing good work amongst the Flatheads; the Pawnees are left without any missionaries at all, and, says the government report, "are probably better off without them." And depreciatory remarks are slightingly introduced concerning the work at other agencies. On the Devil's Lake Agency, the majority of the adults shun the missionaries as they would the gentleman who may be supposed to own the lake by the sides of which they are encamped. The Jesuit fathers and the Catholic sisters are described as working generally with zeal and success, whilst one agency assigned to the Methodists is said to have no religious agency at all. It is to the success of the attempts made to educate the Indians at the public establishments that the philanthropist and humanitarian must look with the most hopefulness.

All the reports of the teachers and visitors of these

schools coincide in one point, that the young Indian is most teachable, and that in respect of acquiring knowledge he is, if anything, the superior of the white, who seems to enjoy no hereditary excellence in his capacity for acquiring knowledge. The Bill to which the Report was an introduction may be considered indeed as the Magna Charta of the Indian tribes if it be followed up by judicious treatment, and careful management of and consideration for the rights conferred upon these tribes as preliminary to their absorption as citizens in the mass of the nation, when they are fit for such an amalgamation with the white races. The advance of the United States westwards has left vacant many military posts and barracks, stranded, as it were, high and dry in the midst of the torrent of civilisation. Fort Bridger, Wyoming; Carlisle Barracks, Pennsylvania; Fort Craig, New Mexico; Fort Cummings, in the same territory, and a number of others, have been named as suitable for the purpose of educating the Indian children; and it was in pursuance of the measure recommended to Congress that the various agencies throughout the Indian Territories were directed to forward children whom their parents might wish to entrust to the officers of the United States for education. "Received in the rudest state of savagism," says the Report, "their progress is already most remarkable." I have already remarked that the health of the boys is not generally satisfactory. Their sanitary condition is bad; and it would appear that sometimes in these long and tedious journeyings from the remote Indian agencies the poor children suffer much.

Even at the present moment the Anglo-Saxon appears to be dealing with the Maori in New Zealand very much as he has dealt with the native in Tasmania and in Australia. The history of our relations with the New Zealand chiefs and people is not in a nature to enable us to throw stones at the Americans with impunity, for the glass house in which we live can very easily be reached. Some sixteen or seventeen years ago a rebellion, arising out of the aggressions of the white settlers on the lands of the Maori, was averted by a Proclamation and by Acts confiscating a large tract of Tallinassey, which became theoretically the property of the Crown. Of course the natives had as little to say to that as the lady who is mentioned in 'Tristram Shandy' had with the declaration that "she was not related to her own child." But they did not recognise the occupancy, and whenever a white man settled upon a portion of the ground they pulled down his fences and removed his landmarks. The contest is still going on, but no one who is acquainted with the history of the colony will doubt what the end will be; and it is coming soon, or it is to come, the moment the colonists are bent upon taking the land, and when it is desired to do so.

"It but feebly expresses the judgment formed from what we have observed to say that we regard the experiment made in this school to educate and improve Indian children as in every way a very remarkable success." *Si sic omnes!* Why does not the United States Government, or if not the Government, the people, abounding in wealth, full of pious impulses, humane, charitable, who justly say that the worst use you can make of an Indian is to hang him; why do not the political economists who declare that it costs a million of dollars to get rid of an Indian with gunpowder and lead; why do not the enterprising and wealthy capitalists who desire to appropriate Indian Reservations all combine to extend the work of these schools so as to absorb all that remains of the Red Man in the rising generation amongst the citizens of the great Republic? A blessed work, worthy of an imperial State, truly great and truly good!

THE END.

LONDON :

PRINTED BY WILLIAM CLOWES AND SONS, LIMITED,

STAMFORD STREET AND CHARING CROSS.

A Catalogue of American and Foreign Books Published or Imported by MESSRS. SAMPSON LOW & CO. can be had on application.

Crown Buildings, 188, Fleet Street, London, January, 1881.

𝔄 Selection from the List of Books

PUBLISHED BY

SAMPSON LOW, MARSTON, SEARLE, & RIVINGTON.

ALPHABETICAL LIST.

A CLASSIFIED *Educational Catalogue of Works* published in Great Britain. Demy 8vo, cloth extra. Second Edition, revised and corrected to Christmas, 1879, 5s.

About Some Fellows. By an ETON BOY, Author of "A Day of my Life." Cloth limp, square 16mo, 2s. 6d.

Adventures of Captain Mago. A Phœnician's Explorations 1000 years B.C. By LEON CAHUN. Numerous Illustrations. Crown 8vo, cloth extra, gilt edges, 7s. 6d.; plainer binding, 5s.

Adventures of a Young Naturalist. By LUCIEN BIART, with 117 beautiful Illustrations on Wood. Edited and adapted by PARKER GILLMORE. Post 8vo, cloth extra, gilt edges, New Edition, 7s. 6d.

Afghan Knife (The). A Novel. By ROBERT ARMITAGE STERNDALE, Author of "Seonee." Small post 8vo, cloth extra, 6s.

After Sundown ; or, The Palette and the Pen. By W. W. FENN, Author of "Blind-Man's Holiday," &c. With Portrait of Author. 2 vols., crown 8vo, cloth extra, 24s.

Albania : A Narrative of Recent Travel. By E. F. KNIGHT. With some very good Illustrations specially made for the work. Crown 8vo, cloth extra, 12s. 6d.

Alcott (Louisa M.) Jimmy's Cruise in the "Pinafore." With 9 Illustrations. Second Edition. Small post 8vo, cloth gilt, 3s. 6d.

—— *Aunt Jo's Scrap-Bag.* Square 16mo, 2s. 6d. (Rose Library, 1s.)

—— *Little Men : Life at Plumfield with Jo's Boys.* Small post 8vo, cloth, gilt edges, 3s. 6d. (Rose Library, Double vol. 2s.)

—— *Little Women.* 1 vol., cloth, gilt edges, 3s. 6d. (Rose Library, 2 vols., 1s. each.)

A

Alcott (Louisa M.) Old-Fashioned Girl. Best Edition, small post 8vo, cloth extra, gilt edges, 3*s.* 6*d.* (Rose Library, 2*s.*)

—— *Work and Beginning Again.* A Story of Experience. 1 vol., small post 8vo, cloth extra, 6*s.* Several Illustrations. (Rose Library, 2 vols., 1*s.* each.)

—— *Shawl Straps.* Small post 8vo, cloth extra, gilt, 3*s.* 6*d.*

—— *Eight Cousins; or, the Aunt Hill.* Small post 8vo, with Illustrations, 3*s.* 6*d.*

—— *The Rose in Bloom.* Small post 8vo, cloth extra, 3*s.* 6*d.*

—— *Silver Pitchers.* Small post 8vo, cloth extra, 3*s.* 6*d.*

—— *Under the Lilacs.* Small post 8vo, cloth extra, 5*s.*

—— *Jack and Jill.* Small post 8vo, cloth extra, 5*s.*

"Miss Alcott's stories are thoroughly healthy, full of racy fun and humour . . . exceedingly entertaining . . . . We can recommend the 'Eight Cousins.'"— *Athenæum.*

Alpine Ascents and Adventures; or, Rock and Snow Sketches. By H. SCHÜTZ WILSON, of the Alpine Club. With Illustrations by WHYMPER and MARCUS STONE. Crown 8vo, 10*s.* 6*d.* 2nd Edition.

Andersen (Hans Christian) Fairy Tales. With Illustrations in Colours by E. V. B. Royal 4to, cloth, 25*s.*

Architecture (The Twenty Styles of). By Dr. W. WOOD, Author of "The Hundred Greatest Men." Imperial 8vo, with 52 Plates.

Art Education. See "Illustrated Text Books."

Autobiography of Sir G. Gilbert Scott, R.A., F.S.A., &c. Edited by his Son, G. GILBERT SCOTT. With an Introduction by the DEAN OF CHICHESTER, and a Funeral Sermon, preached in Westminster Abbey, by the DEAN OF WESTMINSTER. Also, Portrait on steel from the portrait of the Author by G. RICHMOND, R.A. 1 vol., demy 8vo, cloth extra, 18*s.*

THE BAYARD SERIES,

Edited by the late J. HAIN FRISWELL.

Comprising Pleasure Books of Literature produced in the Choicest Style as Companionable Volumes at Home and Abroad.

"We can hardly imagine better books for boys to read or for men to ponder over."—*Times.*

Price 2s. 6d. each Volume, complete in itself, flexible cloth extra, gilt edges, with silk Headbands and Registers.

The Story of the Chevalier Bayard. By M. De Berville.

De Joinville's St. Louis, King of France.

The Essays of Abraham Cowley, including all his Prose Works.

Abdallah; or, The Four Leaves. By Edouard Laboullaye.

The Bayard Series (continued) :—

Table-Talk and Opinions of Napoleon Buonaparte.

Vathek : An Oriental Romance. By William Beckford.

The King and the Commons. A Selection of Cavalier and Puritan Songs. Edited by Professor Morley.

Words of Wellington : Maxims and Opinions of the Great Duke.

Dr. Johnson's Rasselas, Prince of Abyssinia. With Notes.

Hazlitt's Round Table. With Biographical Introduction.

The Religio Medici, Hydriotaphia, and the Letter to a Friend. By Sir Thomas Browne, Knt.

Ballad Poetry of the Affections. By Robert Buchanan.

Coleridge's Christabel, and other

Imaginative Poems. With Preface by Algernon C. Swinburne.

Lord Chesterfield's Letters, Sentences, and Maxims. With Introduction by the Editor, and Essay on Chesterfield by M. de Ste.-Beuve, of the French Academy.

Essays in Mosaic. By Thos. Ballantyne.

My Uncle Toby ; his Story and his Friends. Edited by P. Fitzgerald.

Reflections ; or, Moral Sentences and Maxims of the Duke de la Rochefoucald.

Socrates : Memoirs for English Readers from Xenophon's Memorabilia. By Edw. Levien.

Prince Albert's Golden Precepts.

A Case containing 12 Volumes, price 31s. 6d.; or the Case separately, price 3s. 6d.

Beauty and the Beast. An Old Tale retold, with Pictures by E. V. B. 4to, cloth-extra. 10 Illustrations in Colours. 12s. 6d.

Begum's Fortune (The): A New Story. By JULES VERNE. Translated by W. H. G. KINGSTON. Numerous Illustrations. Crown 8vo, cloth, gilt edges, 7s. 6d. ; plainer binding, plain edges, 5s.

Ben Hur: A Tale of the Christ. By L. WALLACE. Crown 8vo, 6s.

Beumers' German Copybooks. In six gradations at 4d. each.

Biart (Lucien). See "Adventures of a Young Naturalist," "My Rambles in the New World," "The Two Friends," "Involuntary Voyage."

Bickersteth's Hymnal Companion to Book of Common Prayer may be had in various styles and bindings from 1d. to 21s. *Price List and Prospectus will be forwarded on application.*

Bickersteth (Rev. E. H., M.A.) The Reef, and other Parables. 1 vol., square 8vo, with numerous very beautiful Engravings, 2s. 6d.

——— *The Clergyman in his Home.* Small post 8vo, 1s.

——— *The Master's Home-Call; or, Brief Memorials of* Alice Frances Bickersteth. 20th Thousand. 32mo, cloth gilt, 1s.

——— *The Master's Will.* A Funeral Sermon preached on the Death of Mrs. S. Gurney Buxton. Sewn, 6d. ; cloth gilt, 1s.

A 2

Bickersteth (Rev. E. H., M.A.) The Shadow of the Rock. A Selection of Religious Poetry. 18mo, cloth extra, 2s. 6d.

—— *The Shadowed Home and the Light Beyond.* 7th Edition, crown 8vo, cloth extra, 5s.

Biographies of the Great Artists (Illustrated). Each of the following Volumes is illustrated with from twelve to twenty full-page Engravings, printed in the best manner, and bound in ornamental cloth cover, 3s. 6d. Library Edition, bound in a superior style, and handsomely ornamented, with gilt top; six Volumes, enclosed in a cloth case, with lid, £1 11s. 6d. each case.

Hogarth.	Fra Bartolommeo.	Sir David Wilkie.
Turner.	Giotto.	Van Eyck.
Rubens.	Raphael.	Figure Painters of
Holbein.	Van Dyck and Hals.	Holland.
Tintoretto.	Titian.	Michel Angelo.
Little Masters of	Rembrandt.	Delaroche and Vernet.
Germany.	Leonardo da Vinci.	Landseer.
Fra Angelico and	Gainsborough and	Reynolds.
Masaccio.	Constable.	

" Few things in the way of small books upon great subjects, avowedly cheap and necessarily brief, have been hitherto so well done as these biographies of the Great Masters in painting."—*Times.*

" A deserving series."—*Edinburgh Review.*

" Most thoroughly and tastefully edited."—*Spectator.*

Black (Wm.) Three Feathers. Small post 8vo, cloth extra, 6s.

—— *Lady Silverdale's Sweetheart, and other Stories.* 1 vol., small post 8vo, 6s.

—— *Kilmeny: a Novel.* Small post 8vo, cloth, 6s.

—— *In Silk Attire.* 3rd Edition, small post 8vo, 6s.

—— *A Daughter of Heth.* 11th Edition, small post 8vo, 6s.

—— *Sunrise.* 15 Monthly Parts, 1s. each.

Blackmore (R. D.) Lorna Doone. 10th Edition, cr. 8vo, 6s.

—— *Alice Lorraine.* 1 vol., small post 8vo, 6th Edition, 6s.

—— *Clara Vaughan.* Revised Edition, 6s.

—— *Cradock Nowell.* New Edition, 6s.

—— *Cripps the Carrier.* 3rd Edition, small post 8vo, 6s.

—— *Mary Anerley.* New Edition, 6s.

—— *Erema; or, My Father's Sin.* With 12 Illustrations, small post 8vo, 6s.

Blossoms from the King's Garden : Sermons for Children. By the Rev. C. BOSANQUET. 2nd Edition, small post 8vo, cloth extra, 6s.

Blue Banner (The); or, The Adventures of a Mussulman, a Christian, and a Pagan, in the time of the Crusades and Mongol Conquest. Translated from the French of LEON CAHUN. With Seventy-six Wood Engravings. Imperial 16mo, cloth, gilt edges, 7s. 6d.; plainer binding, 5s.

Boy's Froissart (The). 7s. 6d. *See* "Froissart."

Boy's King Arthur (The). With very fine Illustrations.
Square crown 8vo, cloth extra, gilt edges, 7s. 6d. Edited by SIDNEY
LANIER, Editor of "The Boy's Froissart."

Brazil: the Amazons, and the Coast. By HERBERT H. SMITH.
With 115 Full-page and other Illustrations. Demy 8vo, 650 pp., 21s.

Brazil and the Brazilians. By J. C. FLETCHER and D. P.
KIDDER. 9th Edition, Illustrated, 8vo, 21s.

Breton Folk: An Artistic Tour in Brittany. By HENRY
BLACKBURN, Author of "Artists and Arabs," "Normandy Pictu-
resque," &c. With 171 Illustrations by RANDOLPH CALDECOTT.
Imperial 8vo, cloth extra, gilt edges, 21s.

Bricks without Straw. By the Author of "A Fool's Errand."
Crown 8vo, with numerous Illustrations, 7s. 6d.

British Goblins: Welsh Folk-Lore, Fairy Mythology, Legends,
and Traditions. By WIRT SYKES, United States Consul for Wales.
With Illustrations by J. H. THOMAS. This account of the Fairy
Mythology and Folk-Lore of his Principality is, by permission, dedicated to H.R.H. the Prince of Wales. Second Edition. 8vo, 18s.

Buckle (Henry Thomas) The Life and Writings of. By ALFRED
HENRY HUTH. With Portrait. 2 vols.. demy 8vo.

Burnaby (Capt.) See "On Horseback."

Burnham Beeches (Heath, F. G.). With numerous Illustrations
and a Map. Crown 8vo, cloth, gilt edges, 3s. 6d. Second Edition.

Butler (W. F.) The Great Lone Land; an Account of the Red
River Expedition, 1869-70. With Illustrations and Map. Fifth and
Cheaper Edition, crown 8vo, cloth extra, 7s. 6d.

—— *The Wild North Land; the Story of a Winter Journey*
with Dogs across Northern North America. Demy 8vo, cloth, with
numerous Woodcuts and a Map, 4th Edition, 18s. Cr. 8vo, 7s. 6d.

—— *Akim-foo: the History of a Failure.* Demy 8vo, cloth,
2nd Edition, 16s. Also, in crown 8vo, 7s. 6d.

CADOGAN (Lady A.) Illustrated Games of Patience.
Twenty-four Diagrams in Colours, with Descriptive Text. Foolscap
4to, cloth extra, gilt edges, 3rd Edition, 12s. 6d.

Caldecott (R.). See "Breton Folk."

Celebrated Travels and Travellers. See VERNE.

Changed Cross (The), and other Religious Poems. 16mo, 2s. 6d.

Child of the Cavern (The); or, Strange Doings Underground.
By JULES VERNE. Translated by W. H. G. KINGSTON. Numerous
Illustrations. Sq. cr. 8vo, gilt edges, 7s. 6d.; cl., plain edges, 5s.

Child's Play, with 16 Coloured Drawings by E. V. B.   Printed
on thick paper, with tints, 7s. 6d.
———— *New.*   By E. V. B.   Similar to the above.   *See* New.
————— A New and Cheap Edition of the two above, containing 48 Illustrations by E. V. B., printed in tint, handsomely
bound, 3s. 6d.

Children's Lives and How to Preserve Them ; or, The Nursery
Handbook.   By W. Lomas, M.D.   Crown 8vo, cloth, 5s.

Choice Editions of Choice Books.   2s. 6d. each, Illustrated by
C. W. Cope, R.A., T. Creswick, R.A., E. Duncan, Birket
Foster, J. C. Horsley, A.R.A., G. Hicks, R. Redgrave, R.A.,
C. Stonehouse, F. Tayler, G. Thomas, H. J. Townshend,
E. H. Wehnert, Harrison Weir, &c.

Bloomfield's Farmer's Boy.`	Milton's L'Allegro.
Campbell's Pleasures of Hope.	Poetry of Nature. Harrison Weir.
Coleridge's Ancient Mariner.	Rogers' (Sam.) Pleasures of Memory.
Goldsmith's Deserted Village.	Shakespeare's Songs and Sonnets.
Goldsmith's Vicar of Wakefield.	Tennyson's May Queen.
Gray's Elegy in a Churchyard.	Elizabethan Poets.
Keat's Eve of St. Agnes.	Wordsworth's Pastoral Poems.

" Such works are a glorious beatification for a poet."—*Athenæum.*

Christ in Song.   By Dr. Philip Schaff.   A New Edition,
Revised, cloth, gilt edges, 6s.

Cobbett (William).   A Biography.   By Edward Smith.   2
vols., crown 8vo, 25s.

Confessions of a Frivolous Girl (The) : A Novel of Fashionable
Life.   Edited by Robert Grant.   Crown 8vo, 6s.

Cradle-Land of Arts and Creeds ; or, Nothing New under the
Sun.   By Charles J. Stone, Barrister-at-law, and late Advocate,
High Courts, Bombay.   8vo, pp. 420, cloth, 14s.

Cripps the Carrier.   3rd Edition, 6s.   *See* Blackmore.

Cruise of H.M.S. " Challenger" (The).   By W. J. J. Spry, R.N.
With Route Map and many Illustrations.   6th Edition, demy 8vo, cloth,
18s.   Cheap Edition, crown 8vo, some of the Illustrations, 7s. 6d.

Curious Adventures of a Field Cricket.   By Dr. Ernest
Candèze.   Translated by N. D'Anvers.   With numerous fine
Illustrations.   Crown 8vo, gilt, 7s. 6d.; plain binding and edges, 5s.

*D*ANA (*R. H.*) *Two Years before the Mast and Twenty-Four*
years After.   Revised Edition, with Notes, 12mo, 6s.

Daughter (A) of Heth.   By W. Black.   Crown 8vo, 6s.

Day of My Life (A) ; or, Every Day Experiences at Eton.
By an Eton Boy, Author of "About Some Fellows."   16mo, cloth
extra, 2s. 6d.   6th Thousand.

Diane. By Mrs. MACQUOID. Crown 8vo, 6*s.*

Dick Cheveley: his Fortunes and Misfortunes. By W. H. G.
KINGSTON. 350 pp., square 16mo, and 22 full-page Illustrations.
Cloth, gilt edges, 7*s.* 6*d.*; plainer binding, plain edges, 5*s.*

Dick Sands, the Boy Captain. By JULES VERNE. With
nearly 100 Illustrations, cloth, gilt, 10*s.* 6*d.*; plain binding and plain
edges, 5*s.*

Dictionary (General) of Archæology and Antiquities. From
the French of E. BOSC. Crown 8vo, with nearly 200 Illustrations,
10*s.* 6*d.*

Dodge (Mrs. M.) Hans Brinker; or, the Silver Skates. An
entirely New Edition, with 59 Full-page and other Woodcuts.
Square crown 8vo, cloth extra, 5*s.* ; Text only, paper, 1*s.*

Dogs of Assize. A Legal Sketch-Book in Black and White.
Containing 6 Drawings by WALTER J. ALLEN. Folio, in wrapper, 6*s.* 8*d.*

EIGHT Cousins. See ALCOTT.

Eighteenth Century Studies. Essays by F. HITCHMAN.
Demy 8vo, 18*s.*

Elementary Education in Saxony. By J. L. BASHFORD, M.A.,
Trin. Coll., Camb. For Masters and Mistresses of Elementary
Schools. Sewn, 1*s.*

Elinor Dryden. By Mrs. MACQUOID. Crown 8vo, 6*s.*

Embroidery (Handbook of). By L. HIGGIN. Edited by LADY
MARIAN ALFORD, and published by authority of the Royal School of
Art Needlework. With 16 page Illustrations, Designs for Borders,
&c. Crown 8vo, 5*s.*

English Philosophers. Edited by IWAN MULLER, M.A., New
College, Oxon. A Series of Volumes containing short biographies
of the most celebrated English Philosophers, to each of whom is
assigned a separate volume, giving as comprehensive and detailed a
statement of his views and contributions to Philosophy as possible,
explanatory rather than critical, opening with a brief biographical
sketch, and concluding with a short general summary, and a biblio-
graphical appendix. The Volumes will be issued at brief intervals, in
square 16mo, 3*s.* 6*d.*, containing about 200 pp. each.

The following are in the press :—

Bacon. Professor FOWLER, Professor of Logic in Oxford.

Berkeley. Professor T. H. GREEN, Professor of Moral Philosophy,
Oxford.

Hamilton. Professor MONK, Professor of Moral Philosophy, Dublin.
[*Ready.*

J. S. Mill. HELEN TAYLOR, Editor of "The Works of Buckle," &c.

English Philosophers (*continued*) :—

Mansel. Rev. J. H. HUCKIN, D.D., Head Master of Repton.

Adam Smith. ·J. A. FARRER, M.A., Author of "Primitive Manners and Customs." [*Ready.*

Hobbes. A. H. GOSSET, B.A., Fellow of New College, Oxford.

Bentham. G. E. BUCKLE, M.A., Fellow of All Souls', Oxford.

Austin. HARRY JOHNSON, B.A., late Scholar of Queen's College, Oxford.

Hartley. } E. S. BOWEN, B.A., late Scholar of New College,
James Mill. } Oxford.   [*Ready.*

Shaftesbury. } Professor FOWLER.
Hutcheson. }

Arrangements are in progress for volumes on LOCKE, HUME, PALEY, REID, *&c.*

Episodes of French History. Edited, with Notes, Genealogical, Historical, and other Tables, by GUSTAVE MASSON, B.A.

    1. **Charlemagne and the Carlovingians.**
    2. **Louis XI. and the Crusades.**
    3. **Francis I. and Charles V.**
    4. **Francis I. and the Renaissance.**

The above Series is based upon M. Guizot's "History of France." Each volume is choicely Illustrated, with Maps, 2*s.* 6*d.*

Erema ; or, My Father's Sin. *See* BLACKMORE.

Etcher (*The*). Containing 36 Examples of the Original Etched-work of Celebrated Artists, amongst others : BIRKET FOSTER, J. E. HODGSON, R.A., COLIN HUNTER, J. P. HESELTINE, ROBERT W. MACBETH, R. S. CHATTOCK, H. R. ROBERTSON, &c., &c. Imperial 4to, cloth extra, gilt edges, 2*l.* 12*s.* 6*d.*

Eton. *See* "Day of my Life," "Out of School," "About Some Fellows."

Evans (*C.*) *Over the Hills and Far Away.* By C. EVANS. One Volume, crown 8vo, cloth extra, 10*s.* 6*d.*

—— *A Strange Friendship.* Crown 8vo, cloth, 5*s.*

Eve of Saint Agnes (*The*). By JOHN KEATS. Illustrated with Nineteen Etchings by CHARLES O. MURRAY. Folio, cloth extra, 21*s.* An Edition de Luxe on large paper, containing proof impressions, has been printed, and specially bound, 3*l.* 3*s.*

FARM Ballads. By WILL CARLETON. Boards, 1*s.* ; cloth, gilt edges, 1*s.* 6*d.*

Fern Paradise (*The*): *A Plea for the Culture of Ferns.* By F. G. HEATH. New Edition, entirely Rewritten, Illustrated with Eighteen full-page, numerous other Woodcuts, including 8 Plates of Ferns and Four Photographs, large post 8vo, cloth, gilt edges, 12*s.* 6*d.* Sixth Edition. In 12 Parts, sewn, 1*s.* each.

Fern World (The). By F. G. HEATH. Illustrated by Twelve
Coloured Plates, giving complete Figures (Sixty-four in all) of every
Species of British Fern, printed from Nature; by several full-page
Engravings. Cloth, gilt, 6th Edition, 12*s.* 6*d.*
"Mr. HEATH has really given us good, well-written descriptions of our native
Ferns, with indications of their habitats, the conditions under which they grow
naturally, and under which they may be cultivated."—*Athenæum.*

Few (A) Hints on Proving Wills. Enlarged Edition, 1*s.*

First Steps in Conversational French Grammar. By F. JULIEN.
Being an Introduction to "Petites Leçons de Conversation et de
Grammaire," by the same Author. Fcap. 8vo, 128 pp., 1*s.*

Flooding of the Sahara (The). See MACKENZIE.

Food for the People; or, Lentils and other Vegetable Cookery.
By E. E. ORLEBAR. Third Thousand. Small post 8vo, boards, 1*s.*

Fool's Errand (A). By ONE OF THE FOOLS. Author of Bricks
without Straw. Crown 8vo, cloth extra, with numerous Illustrations,
8*s.* 6*d.*

Footsteps of the Master. See STOWE (Mrs. BEECHER).

Forbidden Land (A): Voyages to the Corea. By G. OPPERT.
Numerous Illustrations and Maps. Demy 8vo, cloth extra, 21*s.*

Four Lectures on Electric Induction. Delivered at the Royal
Institution, 1878-9. By J. E. H. GORDON, B.A. Cantab. With
numerous Illustrations. Cloth limp, square 16mo, 3*s.*

Foreign Countries and the British Colonies. Edited by F. S.
PULLING, M.A., Lecturer at Queen's College, Oxford, and formerly
Professor at the Yorkshire College, Leeds. A Series of small Volumes
descriptive of the principal Countries of the World by well-known
Authors, each Country being treated of by a Writer who from
Personal Knowledge is qualified to speak with authority on the Subject.
The Volumes average 180 crown 8vo pages each, contain 2 Maps
and Illustrations, crown 8vo, 3*s.* 6*d.*

The following is a List of the Volumes:—

Denmark and Iceland. By E. C. OTTE, Author of "Scandinavian
History," &c.

Greece. By L. SERGEANT, B.A., Knight of the Hellenic Order
of the Saviour, Author of "New Greece."

Switzerland. By W. A. P. COOLIDGE, M.A., Fellow of
Magdalen College, Editor of *The Alpine Journal.*

Austria. By D. KAY, F.R.G.S.

Russia. By W. R. MORFILL, M.A., Oriel College, Oxford,
Lecturer on the Ilchester Foundation, &c.

Persia. By Major-Gen. Sir F. J. GOLDSMID, K.C.S.I., Author of
"Telegraph and Travel," &c.

Japan. By S. MOSSMAN, Author of "New Japan," &c.

Peru. By CLEMENTS H. MARKHAM, M.A., C.B.

Canada. By W. FRASER RAE, Author of "Westward by
Rail," &c.

Foreign Countries (continued):—

> **Sweden and Norway.** By the Rev. F. H. WOODS, M.A., Fellow of St. John's College, Oxford.
>
> **The West Indies.** By C. H. EDEN, F.R.G.S., Author of "Frozen Asia," &c.
>
> **New Zealand.**
>
> **France.** By Miss M. ROBERTS, Author of "The Atelier du Lys," "Mdlle. Mori," &c.
>
> **Egypt.** By S. LANE POOLE, B.A., Author of "The Life of Edward Lane," &c.
>
> **Spain.** By the Rev. WENTWORTH WEBSTER, M.A., Chaplain at St. Jean de Luz.
>
> **Turkey-in-Asia.** By J. C. McCOAN, M.P.
>
> **Australia.** By J. F. VESEY FITZGERALD, late Premier of New South Wales.
>
> **Holland.** By R. L. POOLE.

Franc (Maude Jeane). The following form one Series, small post 8vo, in uniform cloth bindings, with gilt edges:—

> ——— *Emily's Choice.* 5s.
>
> ——— *Hall's Vineyard.* 4s.
>
> ——— *John's Wife: a Story of Life in South Australia.* 4s.
>
> ——— *Marian; or, the Light of Some One's Home.* 5s.
>
> ——— *Silken Cords and Iron Fetters.* 4s.
>
> ——— *Vermont Vale.* 5s.
>
> ——— *Minnie's Mission.* 4s.
>
> ——— *Little Mercy.* 5s.
>
> ——— *Beatrice Melton's Discipline.* 4s.

Froissart (The Boy's). Selected from the Chronicles of England, France, Spain, &c. By SIDNEY LANIER. The Volume is fully Illustrated, and uniform with "The Boy's King Arthur." Crown 8vo, cloth, 7s. 6d.

GAMES of Patience. See CADOGAN.

Gentle Life (Queen Edition). 2 vols. in 1, small 4to, 10s. 6d.

THE GENTLE LIFE SERIES.

Price 6s. each; or in calf extra, price 10s. 6d.; Smaller Edition, cloth extra, 2s. 6d.

A Reprint (with the exception of "Familiar Words" and "Other People's Windows") has been issued in very neat limp cloth bindings at 2s. 6d. each.

The Gentle Life. Essays in aid of the Formation of Character of Gentlemen and Gentlewomen. 21st Edition.

"Deserves to be printed in letters of gold, and circulated in every house."—*Chambers' Journal.*

The Gentle Life Series (continued):—

About in the World. Essays by Author of "The Gentle Life."
"It is not easy to open it at any page without finding some handy idea."—*Morning Post.*

Like unto Christ. A New Translation of Thomas à Kempis' "De Imitatione Christi." 2nd Edition.
"Could not be presented in a more exquisite form, for a more sightly volume was never seen."—*Illustrated London News.*

Familiar Words. An Index Verborum, or Quotation Handbook. Affording an immediate Reference to Phrases and Sentences that have become embedded in the English language. 4th and enlarged Edition. 6s.
"The most extensive dictionary of quotation we have met with."—*Notes and Queries.*

Essays by Montaigne. Edited and Annotated by the Author of "The Gentle Life." With Portrait. 2nd Edition.
"We should be glad if any words of ours could help to bespeak a large circulation for this handsome attractive book."—*Illustrated Times.*

The Countess of Pembroke's Arcadia. Written by Sir PHILIP SIDNEY. Edited with Notes by Author of "The Gentle Life." 7s. 6d.
"All the best things are retained intact in Mr. Friswell's edition."—*Examiner.*

The Gentle Life. 2nd Series, 8th Edition.
"There is not a single thought in the volume that does not contribute in some measure to the formation of a true gentleman."—*Daily News.*

The Silent Hour: Essays, Original and Selected. By the Author of "The Gentle Life." 3rd Edition.
"All who possess 'The Gentle Life' should own this volume."—*Standard.*

Half-Length Portraits. Short Studies of Notable Persons. By J. HAIN FRISWELL.

Essays on English Writers, for the Self-improvement of Students in English Literature.
"To all who have neglected to read and study their native literature we would certainly suggest the volume before us as a fitting introduction."—*Examiner.*

Other People's Windows. By J. HAIN FRISWELL. 3rd Edition.
"The chapters are so lively in themselves, so mingled with shrewd views of human nature, so full of illustrative anecdotes, that the reader cannot fail to be amused."—*Morning Post.*

A Man's Thoughts. By J. HAIN FRISWELL.

German Primer. Being an Introduction to First Steps in German. By M. T. PREU. 2s. 6d.

Getting On in the World; or, Hints on Success in Life. By W. MATHEWS, LL.D. Small post 8vo, cloth, 2s. 6d.; gilt edges, 3s. 6d.

Gilpin's Forest Scenery. Edited by F. G. HEATH. Large post 8vo, with numerous Illustrations. Uniform with "The Fern World," 12s. 6d. In 6 monthly parts, 2s. each.

Gordon (J. E. H.). See "Four Lectures on Electric Induction," "Physical Treatise on Electricity," &c.

Gouffé. The Royal Cookery Book. By JULES GOUFFÉ; translated and adapted for English use by ALPHONSE GOUFFÉ, Head Pastrycook to her Majesty the Queen. Illustrated with large plates printed in colours. 161 Woodcuts, 8vo, cloth extra, gilt edges, 2*l*. 2*s*.

—— Domestic Edition, half-bound, 10*s*. 6*d*.

"By far the ablest and most complete work on cookery that has ever been submitted to the gastronomical world."—*Pall Mall Gazette.*

Great Artists. See "Biographies."

Great Historic Galleries of England (The). Edited by LORD RONALD GOWER, F.S.A., Trustee of the National Portrait Gallery. Illustrated by 24 large and carefully-executed *permanent* Photographs of some of the most celebrated Pictures by the Great Masters. Imperial 4to, cloth extra, gilt edges, 36*s*.

Great Musicians (The). A Series of Biographies of the Great Musicians. Edited by F HUEFFER.

1. **Wagner.** By the EDITOR.
2. **Weber.** By Sir JULIUS BENEDICT.
3. **Mendelssohn.** By JOSEPH BENNETT.
4. **Schubert.** By H. F. FROST.
5. **Rossini, and the Modern Italian** School. By H. SUTHERLAND EDWARDS.
6. **Marcello.** By ARRIGO BOITO.
7. **Purcell.** By H. W. CUMMINGS.

** Dr. Hiller and other distinguished writers, both English and Foreign, have promised contributions. Each Volume is complete in itself. Small post 8vo, cloth extra, 3*s*.

Guizot's History of France. Translated by ROBERT BLACK. Super-royal 8vo, very numerous Full-page and other Illustrations. In 8 vols., cloth extra, gilt, each 24*s*.

"It supplies a want which has long been felt, and ought to be in the hands of all students of history."—*Times.*

—— —————————— *Masson's School Edition.* The History of France from the Earliest Times to the Outbreak of the Revolution; abridged from the Translation by Robert Black, M.A., with Chronological Index, Historical and Genealogical Tables, &c. By Professor GUSTAVE MASSON, B.A., Assistant Master at Harrow School. With 24 full-page Portraits, and many other Illustrations. 1 vol., demy 8vo, 600 pp., cloth extra, 10*s*. 6*d*.

Guizot's History of England. In 3 vols. of about 500 pp. each, containing 60 to 70 Full-page and other Illustrations, cloth extra, gilt, 24*s*. each.

"For luxury of typography, plainness of print, and beauty of illustration, these volumes, of which but one has as yet appeared in English, will hold their own against any production of an age so luxurious as our own in everything, typography not excepted."—*Times.*

Guyon (Mde.) Life. By UPHAM. 6th Edition, crown 8vo, 6*s*.

*H*ANDBOOK *to the Charities of London. See* LOW's.

———— *of Embroidery ; which see.*

———— *to the Principal Schools of England. See* Practical.

Half-Hours of Blind Man's Holiday ; or, Summer and Winter Sketches in Black and White. By W. W. FENN, Author of "After Sundown," &c. 2 vols., cr. 8vo, 24*s.*

Hall (*W. W.*) *How to Live Long ; or,* 1408 *Health Maxims,* Physical, Mental, and Moral. By W. W. HALL, A.M., M.D. Small post 8vo, cloth, 2*s.* Second Edition.

Hans Brinker ; or, the Silver Skates. See DODGE.

Harper's Monthly Magazine. Published Monthly. 160 pages, fully Illustrated. 1*s.* With two Serial Novels by celebrated Authors.

"'Harper's Magazine' is so thickly sown with excellent illustrations that to count them would be a work of time ; not that it is a picture magazine, for the engravings illustrate the text after the manner seen in some of our choicest *editions de luxe.*"— *St. James's Gazette.*

"It is so pretty, so big, and so cheap. . . . An extraordinary shillingsworth— 160 large octavo pages, with over a score of articles, and more than three times as many illustrations."—*Edinburgh Daily Review.*

"An amazing shillingsworth . . . combining choice literature of both nations."— *Nonconformist.*

Heart of Africa. Three Years' Travels and Adventures in the Unexplored Regions of Central Africa, from 1868 to 1871. By Dr. GEORG SCHWEINFURTH. Numerous Illustrations, and large Map. 2 vols., crown 8vo, cloth, 15*s.*

Heath (*Francis George*). *See* "Fern World," "Fern Paradise," "Our Woodland Trees," "Trees and Ferns," "Gilpin's Forest Scenery," "Burnham Beeches," "Sylvan Spring," &c.

Heber's (*Bishop*) *Illustrated Edition of Hymns.* With upwards of 100 beautiful Engravings. Small 4to, handsomely bound, 7*s.* 6*d.* Morocco, 18*s.* 6*d.* and 21*s.* An entirely New Edition.

Heir of Kilfinnan (*The*). New Story by W. H. G. KINGSTON, Author of "Snow Shoes and Canoes," &c. With Illustrations. Cloth, gilt edges, 7*s.* 6*d.* ; plainer binding, plain edges, 5*s.*

History and Handbook of Photography. Translated from the French of GASTON TISSANDIER. Edited by J. THOMSON. Imperial 16mo, over 300 pages, 70 Woodcuts, and Specimens of Prints by the best Permanent Processes. Second Edition, with an Appendix by the late Mr. HENRY FOX TALBOT. Cloth extra, 6*s.*

History of a Crime (*The*) *; Deposition of an Eye-witness.* By VICTOR HUGO. 4 vols., crown 8vo, 42*s.* Cheap Edition, 1 vol., 6*s.*

———— *Ancient Art.* Translated from the German of JOHN WINCKELMANN, by JOHN LODGE, M.D. With very numerous Plates and Illustrations. 2 vols., 8vo, 36*s.*

———— *England. See* GUIZOT.

———— *France. See* GUIZOT.

History of Russia. See RAMBAUD.
—— *Merchant Shipping.* See LINDSAY.
—— *United States.* See BRYANT.
History and Principles of Weaving by Hand and by Power. With several hundred Illustrations. By ALFRED BARLOW. Royal 8vo, cloth extra, 1*l.* 5*s.* Second Edition.

How I Crossed Africa : from the Atlantic to the Indian Ocean, Through Unknown Countries ; Discovery of the Great Zambesi Affluents, &c.—Vol. I., The King's Rifle. Vol. II., The Coillard Family. By Major SERPA PINTO. With 24 full-page and 118 half-page and smaller Illustrations, 13 small Maps, and 1 large one. 2 vols., demy 8vo, cloth extra, 42*s.*

How to Live Long. See HALL.

How to get Strong and how to Stay so. By WILLIAM BLAIKIE. A Manual of Rational, Physical, Gymnastic, and other Exercises. With Illustrations, small post 8vo, 5*s.*

Hugo (Victor) "Ninety-Three." Illustrated. Crown 8vo, 6*s.*
—— *Toilers of the Sea.* Crown 8vo. Illustrated, 6*s.* ; fancy boards, 2*s.* ; cloth, 2*s.* 6*d.* ; On large paper with all the original Illustrations, 10*s.* 6*d.*
——. *See* "History of a Crime."

Hundred Greatest Men (The). 8 portfolios, 21*s.* each, or 4 vols., half morocco, gilt edges, 12 guineas, containing 15 to 20 Portraits each. See below.

"Messrs. SAMPSON LOW & Co. are about to issue an important 'International' work, entitled, 'THE HUNDRED GREATEST MEN;' being the Lives and Portraits of the 100 Greatest Men of History, divided into Eight Classes, each Class to form a Monthly Quarto Volume. The Introductions to the volumes are to be written by recognized authorities on the different subjects, the English contributors being DEAN STANLEY, Mr. MATTHEW ARNOLD, Mr. FROUDE, and Professor MAX MÜLLER: in Germany, Professor HELMHOLTZ ; in France, MM. TAINE and RENAN ; and in America, Mr. EMERSON. The Portraits are to be Reproductions from fine and rare Steel Engravings."—*Academy.*

Hygiene and Public Health (A Treatise on). Edited by A. H. BUCK, M.D. Illustrated by numerous Wood Engravings. In 2 royal 8vo vols., cloth, one guinea each.

Hymnal Companion to Book of Common Prayer. See BICKERSTETH.

ILLUSTRATED Text-Books of Art-Education. Edited by EDWARD J. POYNTER, R.A. Each Volume contains numerous Illustrations, and is strongly bound for the use of Students, price 5*s.* The Volumes now ready are :—

PAINTING.

Classic and Italian. By PERCY R. HEAD. With 50 Illustrations, 5*s.*

German, Flemish, and Dutch.
French and Spanish.
English and American.

Illustrated Text-Books (continued) :—

ARCHITECTURE.

Classic and Early Christian.
Gothic and Renaissance. By T. ROGER SMITH. With 50 Illustrations, 5s.

SCULPTURE.

Antique: Egyptian and Greek. | Renaissance and Modern.

ORNAMENT.

Decoration in Colour. | Architectural Ornament.

Illustrations of China and its People. By J. THOMPSON, F.R.G.S. Four Volumes, imperial 4to, each 3l. 3s.

In my Indian Garden. By PHIL ROBINSON, Author of " Under the Punkah." With a Preface by EDWIN ARNOLD, M.A., C.S.I., &c. Crown 8vo, limp cloth, 3s. 6d.

Involuntary Voyage (An). Showing how a Frenchman who abhorred the Sea was most unwillingly and by a series of accidents driven round the World. Numerous Illustrations. Square crown 8vo, cloth extra, 7s. 6d.; plainer binding, plain edges, 5s.

Irish Bar. Comprising Anecdotes, Bon-Mots, and Biographical Sketches of the Bench and Bar of Ireland. By J. RODERICK O'FLANAGAN, Barrister-at-Law. Crown 8vo, 12s. Second Edition.

Irish Land Question, and English Public Opinion (The). With a Supplement on Griffith's Valuation. By R. BARRY O'BRIEN, Author of " The Parliamentary History of the Irish Land Question." Fcap. 8vo, cloth, 2s.

Irving (Washington). Complete Library Edition of his Works in 27 Vols., Copyright, Unabridged, and with the Author's Latest Revisions, called the " Geoffrey Crayon " Edition, handsomely printed in large square 8vo, on superfine laid paper, and each volume, of about 500 pages, will be fully Illustrated. 12s. 6d. per vol. *See also* " Little Britain."

JACK and Jill. By Miss ALCOTT. Small post 8vo, cloth, gilt edges, 5s. With numerous Illustrations.

John Holdsworth, Chief Mate. By W. CLARKE RUSSELL, Author of " Wreck of the Grosvenor." Crown 8vo, 6s.

KINGSTON (W. H. G.). See " Snow-Shoes," " Child of the Cavern," " Two Supercargoes," " With Axe and Rifle," " Begum's Fortune," " Heir of Kilfinnan," " Dick Cheveley." Each vol., with very numerous Illustrations, square crown 16mo, gilt edges, 7s. 6d.; plainer binding, plain edges, 5s.

*L*ADY *Silverdale's Sweetheart.* 6s. See BLACK.

Lenten Meditations. In Two Series, each complete in itself. By the Rev. CLAUDE BOSANQUET, Author of "Blossoms from the King's Garden." 16mo, cloth, First Series, 1s. 6d.; Second Series, 2s.

Library of Religious Poetry. A Collection of the Best Poems of all Ages and Tongues. With Biographical and Literary Notes. Edited by PHILIP SCHAFF, D.D., LL.D., and ARTHUR GILMAN, M.A. Royal 8vo, pp. 1036, cloth extra, gilt edges, 21s.

Life and Letters of the Honourable Charles Sumner (*The*). 2 vols., royal 8vo, cloth. Second Edition, 36s.

Lindsay (*W. S.*) *History of Merchant Shipping and Ancient* Commerce. Over 150 Illustrations, Maps, and Charts. In 4 vols., demy 8vo, cloth extra. Vols. 1 and 2, 21s.; vols. 3 and 4, 24s. each.

Little Britain; together with *The Spectre Bridegroom*, and *A* Legend of Sleepy Hollow. By WASHINGTON IRVING. An entirely New *Edition de luxe*, specially suitable for Presentation. Illustrated by 120 very fine Engravings on Wood, by Mr. J. D. COOPER. Designed by Mr. CHARLES O. MURRAY. Square crown 8vo, cloth extra, gilt edges, 10s. 6d.

Little King; or, the Taming of a Young Russian Count. By S. BLANDY. 64 Illustrations. Crown 8vo, gilt edges, 7s. 6d.; plainer binding, 5s.

Little Mercy; or, For Better for Worse. By MAUDE JEANNE FRANC, Author of "Marian," "Vermont Vale," &c., &c. Small post 8vo, cloth extra, 4s. Second Edition.

Lost Sir Massingberd. New Edition, crown 8vo, boards, coloured wrapper, 2s.

Low's German Series—

1. **The Illustrated German Primer.** Being the easiest introduction to the study of German for all beginners. 1s.

2. **The Children's own German Book.** A Selection of Amusing and Instructive Stories in Prose. Edited by Dr. A. L. MEISSNER. Small post 8vo, cloth, 1s. 6d.

3. **The First German Reader, for Children from Ten to** Fourteen. Edited by Dr. A. L. MEISSNER. Small post 8vo, cloth, 1s. 6d.

4. **The Second German Reader.** Edited by Dr. A. L. MEISSNER. Small post 8vo, cloth, 1s. 6d.

   Buchheim's Deutsche Prosa. Two Volumes, sold separately :—

5. **Schiller's Prosa.** Containing Selections from the Prose Works of Schiller, with Notes for English Students. By Dr. BUCHHEIM. Small post 8vo, 2s. 6d.

6. **Goethe's Prosa.** Selections from the Prose Works of Goethe, with Notes for English Students. By Dr. BUCHHEIM. Small post 8vo, 3s. 6d.

Low's International Series of Toy Books. 6*d.* each ; or
Mounted on Linen, 1*s.*

1. **Little Fred and his Fiddle**, from Asbjörnsen's ''Norwegian
   Fairy Tales.''
2. **The Lad and the North Wind**,   ditto.
3. **The Pancake**,   ditto.
4. **The Little Match Girl**, from H. C. Andersen's '' Danish
   Fairy Tales.''
5. **The Emperor's New Clothes**,   ditto.
6. **The Gallant Tin Soldier**,   ditto.

The above in 1 vol., cloth extra, gilt edges, with the whole 36
Coloured Illustrations, 5*s.*

Low's Standard Library of Travel and Adventure. Crown 8vo,
bound uniformly in cloth extra, price 7*s.* 6*d.*

1. **The Great Lone Land.** By Major W. F. BUTLER, C.B.
2. **The Wild North Land.** By Major W. F. BUTLER, C.B.
3. **How I found Livingstone.** By H. M. STANLEY.
4. **The Threshold of the Unknown Region.** By C. R. MARK-
   HAM. (4th Edition, with Additional Chapters, 10*s.* 6*d.*)
5. **A Whaling Cruise to Baffin's Bay and the Gulf of Boothia.**
   By A. H. MARKHAM.
6. **Campaigning on the Oxus.** By J. A. MACGAHAN.
7. **Akim-foo: the History of a Failure.** By MAJOR W. F.
   BUTLER, C.B.
8. **Ocean to Ocean.** By the Rev. GEORGE M. GRANT. With
   Illustrations.
9. **Cruise of the Challenger.** By W. J. J. SPRY, R.N.
10. **Schweinfurth's Heart of Africa.** 2 vols., 15*s.*
11. **Through the Dark Continent.** By H. M. STANLEY. 1 vol.,
    12*s.* 6*d.*

Low's Standard Novels. Crown 8vo, 6*s.* each, cloth extra.

My Lady Greensleeves. By HELEN MATHERS, Authoress of
'' Comin' through the Rye,'' '' Cherry Ripe,'' &c.
Three Feathers. By WILLIAM BLACK.
A Daughter of Heth. 13th Edition. By W. BLACK. With
Frontispiece by F. WALKER, A.R.A.
Kilmeny. A Novel. By W. BLACK.
In Silk Attire. By W. BLACK.
Lady Silverdale's Sweetheart. By W. BLACK.
History of a Crime: The Story of the Coup d'Etat. By VICTOR
HUGO.

Low's Standard Novels (continued) :—

Alice Lorraine. By R. D. BLACKMORE.

Lorna Doone. By R. D. BLACKMORE. 8th Edition.

Cradock Nowell. By R. D. BLACKMORE.

Clara Vaughan. By R. D. BLACKMORE.

Cripps the Carrier. By R. D. BLACKMORE.

Erema; or, My Father's Sin. By R. D. BLACKMORE.

Mary Anerley. By R. D. BLACKMORE.

Innocent. By Mrs. OLIPHANT. Eight Illustrations.

Work. A Story of Experience. By LOUISA M. ALCOTT. Illustrations. *See also* Rose Library.

The Afghan Knife. By R. A. STERNDALE, Author of "Seonee."

A French Heiress in her own Chateau. By the Author of
"One Only," "Constantia," &c. Six Illustrations.

Ninety-Three. By VICTOR HUGO. Numerous Illustrations.

My Wife and I. By Mrs. BEECHER STOWE.

Wreck of the Grosvenor. By W. CLARK RUSSELL.

John Holdsworth (Chief Mate). By W. CLARK RUSSELL.

Elinor Dryden. By Mrs. MACQUOID.

Diane. By Mrs. MACQUOID.

Poganuc People, Their Loves and Lives. By Mrs. BEECHER
STOWE.

A Golden Sorrow. By Mrs. CASHEL HOEY.

A Story of the Dragonnades; or, Asylum Christi. By the Rev.
E. GILLIAT, M.A.

Low's Handbook to the Charities of London. Edited and
revised to date by C. MACKESON, F.S.S., Editor of "A Guide to the
Churches of London and its Suburbs," &c. Paper, 1*s.* ; cloth, 1*s. 6d.*

MACGAHAN (J. A.) Campaigning on the Oxus, and the
Fall of Khiva. With Map and numerous Illustrations, 4th Edition,
small post 8vo, cloth extra, 7*s. 6d.*

Macgregor (John) "Rob Roy" on the Baltic. 3rd Edition,
small post 8vo, 2*s. 6d.* ; cloth, gilt edges, 3*s. 6d.*

—— *A Thousand Miles in the "Rob Roy" Canoe.* 11th
Edition, small post 8vo, 2*s. 6d,* ; cloth, gilt edges, 3*s. 6d.*

—— *Description of the "Rob Roy" Canoe,* with Plans,
&c., 1*s.*

—— *The Voyage Alone in the Yawl "Rob Roy."* New
Edition, thoroughly revised, with additions, small post 8vo, 5*s.* ;
boards, 2*s. 6d.*

Mackenzie (D.) The Flooding of the Sahara. By DONALD
MACKENZIE. 8vo, cloth extra, with Illustrations, 10*s*. 6*d*.

Macquoid (Mrs.) Elinor Dryden. Crown 8vo, cloth, 6*s*.

—— *Diane.* Crown 8vo, 6*s*.

Magazine. See HARPER.

Markham (C. R.) The Threshold of the Unknown Region.
Crown 8vo, with Four Maps, 4th Edition. Cloth extra, 10*s*. 6*d*.

Maury (Commander) Physical Geography of the Sea, and its
Meteorology. Being a Reconstruction and Enlargement of his formei
Work, with Charts and Diagrams. New Edition, crown 8vo, 6*s*.

Memoirs of Count Miot de Melito. 2 vols., demy 8vo, 36*s*.

Memoirs of Madame de Rémusat, 1802—1808. By hei Grandson, M. PAUL DE RÉMUSAT, Senator. Translated by Mrs. CASHEL
HOEY and Mr. JOHN LILLIE. 4th Edition, cloth extra. This
work was written by Madame de Rémusat during the time she
was living on the most intimate terms with the Empress Josephine,
and is full of revelations respecting the private life of Bonaparte, and
of men and politics of the first years of the century. Revelations
which have already created a great sensation in Paris. 8vo, 2 vols., 32*s*.

Menus (366, *one for each day of the year*). Translated from the
French of COUNT BRISSE, by Mrs. MATTHEW CLARKE. Crown
8vo, 10*s*. 6*d*.

Men of Mark : a Gallery of Contemporary Portraits of the most
Eminent Men of the Day taken from Life, especially for this publication, price 1*s*. 6*d*. monthly. Vols. I., II., III., IV., and V., handsomely bound, cloth, gilt edges, 25*s*. each.

Mendelssohn Family (The). Translated from the German of
E. BOCK. Demy 8vo, 16*s*.

Michael Strogoff. 10*s*. 6*d*. and 5*s*. *See* VERNE.

Mitford (Miss). See " Our Village."

Military Maxims. By CAPTAIN B. TERLING. Medium 16mo,
in roan case, with pencil for the pocket, 10*s*. 6*d*.

Mountain and Prairie : a Journey from Victoria to Winnipeg,
vid Peace River Pass. By the Rev. DANIEL M. GORDON, B.D.,
Ottawa. Small post 8vo, with Maps and Illustrations, cloth extra,
8*s*. 6*d*.

Music. See " Great Musicians."

My Lady Greensleeves. By HELEN MATHERS, Authoress of
" Comin' through the Rye," " Cherry Ripe," &c. 1 vol. edition,
crown 8vo, cloth, 6*s*.

Mysterious Island. By JULES VERNE. 3 vols., imperial 16mo.
150 Illustrations, cloth gilt, 3*s.* 6*d.* each; elaborately bound, gilt
edges, 7*s.* 6*d.* each. Cheap Edition, with some of the Illustrations,
cloth, gilt, 2*s.*; paper, 1*s.* each.

NATIONAL Music of the World. By the late HENRY F.
CHORLEY. Edited by H. G. HEWLETT. Crown 8vo, cloth, 8*s.* 6*d.*

Naval Brigade in South Africa (The). By HENRY F. NOR-
BURY, C.B., R.N. Crown 8vo, cloth extra, 10*s.* 6*d.*

New Child's Play (A). Sixteen Drawings by E. V. B. Beautifully printed in colours, 4to, cloth extra, 12*s.* 6*d.*

New Guinea (A Few Months in). By OCTAVIUS C. STONE,
F.R.G.S. With numerous Illustrations from the Author's own
Drawings. Crown 8vo, cloth, 12*s.*

—————— *What I did and what I saw.* By L. M. D'ALBERTIS,
Officer of the Order of the Crown of Italy, Honorary Member and
Gold Medallist of the I.R.G.S., C.M.Z.S., &c., &c. In 2 vols.,
demy 8vo, cloth extra, with Maps, Coloured Plates, and numerous
very fine Woodcut Illustrations, 42*s.*

New Ireland. By A. M. SULLIVAN, M.P. for Louth. 2 vols.,
demy 8vo, 30*s.* Cheaper Edition, 1 vol., crown 8vo, 8*s.* 6*d.*

New Novels. Crown 8vo, cloth, 10*s.* 6*d.* per vol. :—

Mary Marston. By GEORGE MACDONALD. 3 vols. Third Edition.
Sarah de Beranger. By JEAN INGELOW. 3 vols.
Don John. By JEAN INGELOW. 3 vols.
Sunrise : A Story of these Times. By WILLIAM BLACK. 3 vols.
A Sailor's Sweetheart. By W. CLARK RUSSELL, Author of "The
   Wreck of the Grosvenor," "John Holdsworth," &c. 3 vols.
Lisa Lena. By EDWARD JENKINS, Author of "Ginx's Baby."
   2 vols.
A Plot of the Present Day. By KATE HOPE. 3 vols.
Black Abbey. By M. CROMMELIN, Author of "Queenie," &c.
   3 vols.
Flower o' the Broom. By the Author of "Rare Pale Margaret,"
   3 vols.
The Grandidiers : A Tale of Berlin. Translated from the German
   by Captain WM. SAVILE. 3 vols.
Errant : A Life Story of Latter-Day Chivalry. By PERCY GREG,
   Author of "Across the Zodiac," &c. 3 vols.
Fancy Free. By C. GIBBON. 3 vols.
The Stillwater Tragedy. By J. B. ALDRICH.
Prince Fortune and Prince Fatal. By Mrs. CARRINGTON,
   Author of "My Cousin Maurice," &c. 3 vols.

New Novels (continued) :—

An English Squire. By C. B. COLERIDGE, Author of "Lady
Betty," "Hanbury Wills," &c. 3 vols.
Christowell. By R. D. BLACKMORE. 3 vols.
Mr. Caroli. By Miss SEGUIN. 3 vols.
David Broome, Artist. By Miss O'REILLY. 3 vols.
Braes of Yarrow. By CHAS. GIBBON. 3 vols.

Nice and Her Neighbours. By the Rev. CANON HOLE, Author
of "A Book about Roses," "A Little Tour in Ireland," &c. Small
4to, with numerous choice Illustrations, 12*s.* 6*d.*

Noble Words and Noble Deeds. From the French of E. MULLER.
Containing many Full-page Illustrations by PHILIPPOTEAUX. Square
imperial 16mo, cloth extra, 7*s.* 6*d.* ; plainer binding, plain edges, 5*s.*

North American Review (The). Monthly, price 2*s.* 6*d.*

Nothing to Wear ; and Two Millions. By W. A. BUTLER.
New Edition. Small post 8vo, in stiff coloured wrapper, 1*s.*

Nursery Playmates (Prince of). 217 Coloured pictures for
Children by eminent Artists. Folio, in coloured boards, 6*s.*

*O*BERAMMERGAU *Passion Play.* See "Art in the
Mountains."

O'Brien. See "Parliamentary History" and "Irish Land
Question."

Old-Fashioned Girl. See ALCOTT.

On Horseback through Asia Minor. By Capt. FRED BURNABY,
Royal Horse Guards, Author of "A Ride to Khiva." 2 vols.,
8vo, with three Maps and Portrait of Author, 6th Edition, 38*s.* ;
Cheaper Edition, crown 8vo, 10*s.* 6*d.*

Our Little Ones in Heaven. Edited by the Rev. H. ROBBINS.
With Frontispiece after Sir JOSHUA REYNOLDS. Fcap., cloth extra,
New Edition—the 3rd, with Illustrations, 5*s.*

Our Village. By MARY RUSSELL MITFORD. Illustrated with
Frontispiece Steel Engraving, and 12 full-page and 157 smaller Cuts
of Figure Subjects and Scenes. Crown 4to, cloth, gilt edges, 21*s.*

Our Woodland Trees. By F. G. HEATH. Large post 8vo,
cloth, gilt edges, uniform with "Fern World" and "Fern Paradise,"
by the same Author. 8 Coloured Plates (showing leaves of every
British Tree) and 20 Woodcuts, cloth, gilt edges, 12*s.* 6*d.* Third
Edition.

PAINTERS of All Schools. By LOUIS VIARDOT, and other Writers. 500 pp., super-royal 8vo, 20 Full-page and 70 smaller Engravings, cloth extra, 25s. A New Edition is issued in Half-crown parts, with fifty additional portraits, cloth, gilt edges, 31s. 6d.

Painting (A Short History of the British School of). By GEO. H. SHEPHERD. Post 8vo, cloth, 3s. 6d.

Palliser (Mrs.) A History of Lace, from the Earliest Period. A New and Revised Edition, with additional cuts and text, upwards of 100 Illustrations and coloured Designs. 1 vol., 8vo, 1l. 1s.

—— *Historic Devices, Badges, and War Cries.* 8vo, 1l. 1s.

—— *The China Collector's Pocket Companion.* With upwards of 1000 Illustrations of Marks and Monograms. 2nd Edition, with Additions. Small post 8vo, limp cloth, 5s.

Parliamentary History of the Irish Land Question (The). From 1829 to 1869, and the Origin and Results of the Ulster Custom. By R. BARRY O'BRIEN, Barrister-at-Law, Author of "The Irish Land Question and English Public Opinion." 3rd Edition, corrected and revised, with additional matter. Post 8vo, cloth extra, 6s.

The Right Hon. W. E. GLADSTONE, M.P., in a Letter to the Author, says:— "I thank you for kindly sending me your work, and I hope that the sad and discreditable story which you have told so well in your narrative of the Irish Land Question may be useful at a period when we have more than ever of reason to desire that it should be thoroughly understood."

Pathways of Palestine: a Descriptive Tour through the Holy Land. By the Rev. CANON TRISTRAM. Illustrated with 44 permanent Photographs. (The Photographs are large, and most perfect Specimens of the Art.) Published in 22 Monthly Parts, 4to, in Wrapper, 2s. 6d. each.

". . . The Photographs which illustrate these pages may justly claim, as works of art, to be the most admirably executed views which have been produced. . . . "As the writer is on the point of making a fourth visit of exploration to the country, any new discoveries which come under observation will be at once incorporated in this work."

Peasant Life in the West of England. By FRANCIS GEORGE HEATH, Author of "Sylvan Spring," "The Fern World." Crown 8vo, about 350 pp., 10s. 6d.

Petites Leçons de Conversation et de Grammaire: Oral and Conversational Method; being Lessons introducing the most Useful Topics of Conversation, upon an entirely new principle, &c. By F. JULIEN, French Master at King Edward the Sixth's School, Birmingham. Author of "The Student's French Examiner," "First Steps in Conversational French Grammar," which see.

Phillips (L.) Dictionary of Biographical Reference. 8vo, 1l. 11s. 6d.

Photography (History and Handbook of). See TISSANDIER.

Physical Treatise on Electricity and Magnetism. By J. E. H. GORDON, B.A. With about 200 coloured, full-page, and other Illustrations. Among the newer portions of the work may be enumerated : All the more recent investigations on Striæ by Spottis-woode, De la Rue, Moulton, &c., an account of Mr. Crooke's recent researches ; full descriptions and pictures of all the modern Magnetic Survey Instruments now used at Kew Observatory ; full accounts of all the modern work on Specific Inductive Capacity, and of the more recent determination of the ratio of Electric units (v). In respect to the number and beauty of the Illustrations, the work is quite unique. 2 vols., 8vo, 36s.

Pinto (Major Serpa). *See* "How I Crossed Africa."

Plutarch's Lives. An Entirely New and Library Edition. Edited by A. H. CLOUGH, Esq. 5 vols., 8vo, 2l. 10s.; half-morocco, gilt top, 3l. Also in 1 vol., royal 8vo, 800 pp., cloth extra, 18s.; half-bound, 21s.

Poems of the Inner Life. A New Edition, Revised, with many additional Poems. Small post 8vo, cloth, 5s.

Poganuc People: their Loves and Lives. By Mrs. BEECHER STOWE. Crown 8vo, cloth, 6s.

Polar Expeditions. *See* KOLDEWEY, MARKHAM, MACGAHAN, and NARES.

Poynter (Edward J., R.A.). *See* "Illustrated Text-books."

Practical (A) Handbook to the Principal Schools of England. By C. E. PASCOE. New Edition, crown 8vo, cloth extra, 3s. 6d.

*Prejevalsky (N. M.) From Kulja, across the Tian Shan to Lob-*nor. Translated by E. DELMAR MORGAN, F.R.G.S. Demy 8vo, with a Map. 16s.

Primitive Folk Moots ; or, Open-Air Assemblies in Britain. By GEORGE LAURENCE GOMME, F.S.A., Honorary Secretary to the Folk-Lore Society, Author of " Index of Municipal Offices." 1 vol., crown 8vo, cloth, 12s.
    This work deals with an earlier phase of the history of English Institutions than has yet been attempted.

Publishers' Circular (The), and General Record of British and Foreign Literature. Published on the 1st and 15th of every Month, 3d.

Pyrenees (The). By HENRY BLACKBURN. With 100 Illustra-tions by GUSTAVE DORE, a New Map of Routes, and Information for Travellers, corrected to 1881. With a description of Lourdes in 1880. Crown 8vo, cloth extra, 7s. 6d.

*R*AMBAUD *(Alfred).   History of Russia, from its Origin*
to the Year 1877. With Six Maps. Translated by Mrs. L. B.
LAN.2 vols., demy 8vo, cloth extra, 38*s.*

Recollections of Writers.   By CHARLES and MARY COWDEN
CLARKE. Authors of " The Concordance to Shakespeare," &c. ;
with Letters of CHARLES LAMB, LEIGH HUNT, DOUGLAS JERROLD,
and CHARLES DICKENS ; and a Preface by MARY COWDEN CLARKE.
Crown 8vo, cloth, 10*s. 6d.*

Rémusat (Madame de).   See " Memoirs of."

Robinson (Phil).   See " In my Indian Garden," " Under the
Punkah."

Rochefoucauld's Reflections.   Bayard Series, 2*s. 6d.*

Rogers (S.)   Pleasures of Memory.   See " Choice Editions of
Choice Books." 2*s. 6d.*

Rose in Bloom.   See ALCOTT.

The Rose Library.   Popular Literature of all countries.   Each
volume, 1*s.* ; cloth, 2*s. 6d.* Many of the Volumes are Illustrated—

1. **Sea-Gull Rock.** By JULES SANDEAU. Illustrated.
2. **Little Women.** By LOUISA M. ALCOTT.
3. **Little Women Wedded.** Forming a Sequel to "Little Women."
4. **The House on Wheels.** By MADAME DE STOLZ. Illustrated.
5. **Little Men.** By LOUISA M. ALCOTT. Dble. vol., 2*s.* ; cloth, 3*s. 6d.*
6. **The Old-Fashioned Girl.** By LOUISA M. ALCOTT. Double
     vol., 2*s.* ; cloth, 3*s. 6d.*
7. **The Mistress of the Manse.** By J. G. HOLLAND.
8. **Timothy Titcomb's Letters to Young People, Single and
     Married.**
9. **Undine, and the Two Captains.** By Baron DE LA MOTTE
     FOUQUÉ. A New Translation by F. E. BUNNETT. Illustrated.
10. **Draxy Miller's Dowry, and the Elder's Wife.** By SAXE
      HOLM.
11. **The Four Gold Pieces.** By Madame GOURAUD. Numerous
      Illustrations.
12. **Work.** A Story of Experience. First Portion. By LOUISA M.
      ALCOTT.
13. **Beginning Again.** Being a Continuation of "Work." By
      LOUISA M. ALCOTT.
14. **Picciola; or, the Prison Flower.** By X. B. SAINTINE.
      Numerous Graphic Illustrations.

The Rose Library (*continued*) :—

15. **Robert's Holidays.** Illustrated.
16. **The Two Children of St. Domingo.** Numerous Illustrations.
17. **Aunt Jo's Scrap Bag.**
18. **Stowe (Mrs. H. B.) The Pearl of Orr's Island.**
19. ———— **The Minister's Wooing.**
20. ———— **Betty's Bright Idea.**
21. ———— **The Ghost in the Mill.**
22. ———— **Captain Kidd's Money.**
23. ———— **We and our Neighbours.** Double vol., 2*s.*
24. ———— **My Wife and I.** Double vol., 2*s.* ; cloth, gilt, 3*s.* 6*d.*
25. **Hans Brinker ; or, the Silver Skates.**
26. **Lowell's My Study Window.**
27. **Holmes (O. W.) The Guardian Angel.**
28. **Warner (C. D.) My Summer in a Garden.**
29. **Hitherto.** By the Author of "The Gayworthys." 2 vols., 1*s.* each.
30. **Helen's Babies.** By their Latest Victim.
31. **The Barton Experiment.** By the Author of "Helen's Babies."
32. **Dred.** By Mrs. BEECHER STOWE. Double vol., 2*s.* ; cloth, gilt, 3*s.* 6*d.*
33. **Warner (C. D.) In the Wilderness.**
34. **Six to One.** A Seaside Story.
35. **Nothing to Wear, and Two Millions.**
36. **Farm Ballads.** By WILL CARLETON.

Russell (*W. Clarke*). *See* "A Sailor's Sweetheart," 3 vols., 31*s.* 6*d.* ; "Wreck of the Grosvenor," 6*s.* ; "John Holdsworth (Chief Mate)," 6*s.*

Russell (*W. H., LL.D.*) *The Tour of the Prince of Wales in* India. By W. H. RUSSELL, LL.D. Fully Illustrated by SYDNEY P. HALL, M.A. Super-royal 8vo, cloth extra, gilt edges, 52*s.* 6*d.* ; Large Paper Edition, 84*s.*

SANCTA Christina : a Story of the First Century. By ELEANOR E. ORLEBAR. With a Preface by the Bishop of Winchester. Small post 8vo, cloth extra, 5*s.*

Seonee : Sporting in the Satpura Range of Central India, and in the Valley of the Nerbudda. By R. A. STERNDALE, F.R.G.S. 8vo, with numerous Illustrations, 21*s.*

Seven Years in South Africa : Travels, Researches, and Hunting Adventures between the Diamond-Fields and the Zambesi (1872—1879). By Dr. EMIL HOLUB. With over 100 Original Illustrations and 4 Maps. In 2 vols., demy 8vo, cloth extra, 42*s.*

Serpent Charmer (The): *a Tale of the Indian Mutiny.* By LOUIS ROUSSELET, Author of "India and its Native Princes." Numerous Illustrations. Crown 8vo, cloth extra, gilt edges, 7*s.* 6*d.* ; plainer binding, 5*s.*

Shakespeare (The Boudoir). Edited by HENRY CUNDELL. Carefully bracketted for reading aloud ; freed from all objectionable matter, and altogether free from notes. Price 2*s.* 6*d.* each volume, cloth extra, gilt edges. Contents :—Vol I., Cymbeline—Merchant of Venice. Each play separately, paper cover, 1*s.* Vol. II., As You Like It—King Lear—Much Ado about Nothing. Vol. III., Romeo and Juliet—Twelfth Night—King John. The latter six plays separately, paper cover, 9*d.*

Shakespeare Key (The). Forming a Companion to "The Complete Concordance to Shakespeare." By CHARLES and MARY COWDEN CLARKE. Demy 8vo, 800 pp., 21*s.*

Shooting: its Appliances, Practice, and Purpose. By JAMES DALZIEL DOUGALL, F.S.A., F.Z.A., Author, of "Scottish Field Sports," &c. Crown 8vo, cloth extra, 10*s.* 6*d.*

"The book is admirable in every way. . . . . We wish it every success."—*Globe.*
"A very complete treatise. . . . . Likely to take high rank as an authority on shooting."—*Daily News.*

Silent Hour (The). *See* "Gentle Life Series."

Silver Pitchers. *See* ALCOTT.

Simon (Jules). *See* "Government of M. Thiers."

Six to One. A Seaside Story. 16mo, boards, 1*s.*

Smith (G.) Assyrian Explorations and Discoveries. By the late GEORGE SMITH. Illustrated by Photographs and Woodcuts. Demy 8vo, 6th Edition, 18*s.*

—— *The Chaldean Account of Genesis.* By the late G. SMITH, of the Department of Oriental Antiquities, British Museum. With many Illustrations. Demy 8vo, cloth extra, 6th Edition, 16*s.*

—— An entirely New Edition, completely revised and re-written by the Rev. PROFESSOR SAYCE, Queen's College, Oxford. Demy 8vo, 18*s.*

Snow-Shoes and Canoes; or, the Adventures of a Fur-Hunter in the Hudson's Bay Territory. By W. H. G. KINGSTON. 2nd Edition. With numerous Illustrations. Square crown 8vo, cloth extra, gilt edges, 7*s.* 6*d.* ; plainer binding, 5*s.*

Songs and Etchings in Shade and Sunshine. By J. E. G.
Illustrated with 44 Etchings. Small 4to, cloth, gilt tops, 25*s.*

South African Campaign, 1879 (*The*). Compiled by J. P.
MACKINNON (formerly 72nd Highlanders), and S. H. SHADBOLT;
and dedicated, by permission, to Field-Marshal H.R.H. The Duke
of Cambridge. 4to, handsomely bound in cloth extra, 2*l.* 10*s.*

South Kensington Museum. Published, with the sanction of
the Science and Art Department, in Monthly Parts, each containing 8 Plates, price 1*s.* Volume I., containing 12 numbers, handsomely bound, 16*s.*

Stanley (H. M.) How I Found Livingstone. Crown 8vo, cloth
extra, 7*s.* 6*d.* ; large Paper Edition, 10*s.* 6*d.*

—— *"My Kalulu," Prince, King, and Slave.* A Story
from Central Africa. Crown 8vo, about 430 pp., with numerous graphic
Illustrations, after Original Designs by the Author. Cloth, 7*s.* 6*d.*

—— *Coomassie and Magdala.* A Story of Two British
Campaigns in Africa. Demy 8vo, with Maps and Illustrations, 16*s.*

—— *Through the Dark Continent,* which see.

Story of a Mountain (*The*). By E. RECLUS. Translated by
BERTHA NESS. 8vo, with Illustrations, cloth extra, gilt edges,
7*s.* 6*d.*

Story of a Soldier's Life (*The*) ; or, *Peace, War, and Mutiny.*
By Lieut.-General JOHN ALEXANDER EWART, C.B., Aide-de-Camp
to the Queen from 1859 to 1872. 2 vols., demy 8vo, with Illustrations. •

Story of the Zulu Campaign (*The*). By Major ASHE (late
King's Dragoon Guards), and Captain the Hon. E. V. WYATT-
EDGELL (late 17th Lancers, killed at Ulundi). Dedicated by special
permission to Her Imperial Highness the Empress Eugénie. 8vo, 16*s.* •

Story without an End. From the German of Carové, by the late
Mrs. SARAH T. AUSTIN. Crown 4to, with 15 Exquisite Drawings
by E. V. B., printed in Colours in Fac-simile of the original Water
Colours; and numerous other Illustrations. New Edition, 7*s.* 6*d.*

—— square 4to, with Illustrations by HARVEY. 2*s.* 6*d.*

Stowe (Mrs. Beecher) Dred. Cheap Edition, boards, 2*s.* Cloth,
gilt edges, 3*s.* 6*d.*

Stowe (Mrs. Beecher) Footsteps of the Master. With Illustrations and red borders. Small post 8vo, cloth extra, 6s.

—— *Geography,* with 60 Illustrations. Square cloth, 4s. 6d.

—— *Little Foxes.* Cheap Edition, 1s.; Library Edition, 4s. 6d.

—— *Betty's Bright Idea.* 1s.

—— *My Wife and I; or, Harry Henderson's History.* Small post 8vo, cloth extra, 6s.*

—— *Minister's Wooing.* 5s.; Copyright Series, 1s. 6d.; cl., 2s.*

—— *Old Town Folk.* 6s.; Cheap Edition, 2s. 6d.

—— *Old Town Fireside Stories.* Cloth extra, 3s. 6d.

—— *Our Folks at Poganuc.* 10s. 6d.

—— *We and our Neighbours.* 1 vol., small post 8vo, 6s. Sequel to "My Wife and I."*

—— *Pink and White Tyranny.* Small post 8vo, 3s. 6d. Cheap Edition, 1s. 6d. and 2s.

—— *Queer Little People.* 1s.; cloth, 2s.

—— *Chimney Corner.* 1s.; cloth, 1s. 6d.

—— *The Pearl of Orr's Island.* Crown 8vo, 5s.*

—— *Little Pussey Willow.* Fcap., 2s.

—— *Woman in Sacred History.* Illustrated with 15 Chromo-lithographs and about 200 pages of Letterpress. Dem 4to, cloth extra, gilt edges, 25s.

Student's French Examiner. By F. JULIEN, Author of " Petites Leçons de Conversation et de Grammaire." Square crown 8vo, cloth, 2s

Studies in German Literature. By BAYARD TAYLOR. Edited by MARIE TAYLOR. With an Introduction by the Hon. GEORGE H. BOKER. 8vo, cloth extra, 10s. 6d.

* *See also* Rose Library.

Studies in the Theory of Descent. By Dr. AUG. WEISMANN, Professor in the University of Freiburg. Translated and edited by RAPHAEL MELDOLA, F.C.S., Secretary of the Entomological Society of London. Part I.—"On the Seasonal Dimorphism of Butterflies," containing Original Communications by Mr. W. H. EDWARDS, of Coalburgh. With two Coloured Plates. Price of Part. I. (to Subscribers for the whole work only), 8*s*; Part II. (6 coloured plates), 16*s*. ; Part III., 6*s*.

Sugar Beet (The). Including a History of the Beet Sugar Industry in Europe, Varieties of the Sugar Beet, Examination, Soils, Tillage, Seeds and Sowing, Yield and Cost of Cultivation, Harvesting, Transportation, Conservation, Feeding Qualities of the Beet and of the Pulp, &c. By L. S. WARE. Illustrated. 8vo, cloth extra, 21*s*.

Sullivan (A. M., M.P.). See "New Ireland."

Sulphuric Acid (A Practical Treatise on the Manufacture of). By A. G. and C. G. LOCK, Consulting Chemical Engineers. With 77 Construction Plates, and other Illustrations. Royal 8vo, 2*l*. 12*s*. 6*d*.

Sumner (Hon. Charles). See Life and Letters.

Sunrise: A Story of These Times. By WILLIAM BLACK, Author of "A Daughter of Heth," &c. 3 vols., 31*s*. 6*d*.

Surgeon's Handbook on the Treatment of Wounded in War. By Dr. FRIEDRICH ESMARCH, Professor of Surgery in the University of Kiel, and Surgeon-General to the Prussian Army. Translated by H. H. CLUTTON, B.A. Cantab, F.R.C.S. Numerous Coloured Plates and Illustrations, 8vo, strongly bound in flexible leather, 1*l*. 8*s*.

Sylvan Spring. By FRANCIS GEORGE HEATH. Illustrated by 12 Coloured Plates, drawn by F. E. HULME, F.L.S., Artist and Author of "Familiar Wild Flowers;" by 16 full-page, and more than 100 other Wood Engravings. Large post 8vo, cloth, gilt edges, 12*s*. 6*d*.

TAUCHNITZ'S English Editions of German Authors. Each volume, cloth flexible, 2*s*. ; or sewed, 1*s*. 6*d*. (Catalogues post free on application.)

—— *(B.) German and English Dictionary.* Cloth, 1*s*. 6*d*.; roan, 2*s*,

—— *French and English.* Paper, 1*s*. 6*d*.; cloth, 2*s*. ; roan 2*s*. 6*d*.

Tauchnitz (B.) Italian and English Dictionary. Paper, 1s. 6d.; cloth, 2s. ; roan, 2s. 6d.

———— *Spanish and English.* Paper, 1s. 6d. ; cloth, 2s. ; roan, 2s. 6d.

———— *New Testament.* Cloth, 2s. ; gilt, 2s. 6d.

Taylor (Bayard). *See* "Studies in German Literature."

Through America ; or, Nine Months in the United States. By W. G. MARSHALL, M.A. With nearly 100 Woodcuts of Views of Utah country and the famous Yosemite Valley ; The Giant Trees, New York, Niagara, San Francisco, &c.; containing a full account of Mormon Life, as noted by the Author during his visits to Salt Lake City in 1878 and 1879. In 1 vol., demy 8vo, 21s.

Through the Dark Continent : The Sources of the Nile ; Around the Great Lakes, and down the Congo. By HENRY M. STANLEY. 2 vols., demy 8vo, containing 150 Full-page and other Illustrations, 2 Portraits of the Author, and 10 Maps, 42s. Seventh Thousand. Cheaper Edition, crown 8vo, with some of the Illustrations and Maps. 1 vol., 12s. 6d.

Tour of the Prince of Wales in India. *See* RUSSELL.

Trees and Ferns. By F. G. HEATH. Crown 8vo, cloth, gilt edges, with numerous Illustrations, 3s. 6d.

Two Friends. By LUCIEN BIART, Author of "Adventures of a Young Naturalist," "My Rambles in the New World," &c. Small post 8vo, numerous Illustrations, gilt edges, 7s. 6d. ; plainer binding, 5s.

Two Supercargoes (The) ; or, Adventures in Savage Africa. By W. H. G. KINGSTON. Numerous Full-page Illustrations. Square imperial 16mo, cloth extra, gilt edges, 7s. 6d. ; plainer binding, 5s.

UNDER the Punkah. By PHIL ROBINSON, Author of "In my Indian Garden." Crown 8vo, limp cloth, uniform with the above, 3s. 6d.

Up and Down ; or, Fifty Years' Experiences in Australia, California, New Zealand, India, China, and the South Pacific. Being the Life History of Capt. W. J. BARRY. Written by Himself. With several Illustrations. Crown 8vo, cloth extra, 8s. 6d.

BOOKS BY JULES VERNE.

LARGE CROWN 8vo . . .	Containing 350 to 600 pp. and from 50 to 100 full-page illustrations.		Containing the whole of the text with some illustrations.	
WORKS.	In very handsome cloth binding, gilt edges.	In plainer binding, plain edges.	In cloth binding, gilt edges, smaller type.	Coloured Boards.
	s. d.	*s. d.*	*s. d.*	
Twenty Thousand Leagues under the Sea. Part I. Ditto. Part II.	10 6	5 0	3 6	2 vols., 1s. each.
Hector Servadac . . .	10 6	5 0		
The Fur Country . . .	10 6	5 0	3 6	2 vols., 1s. each.
From the Earth to the Moon and a Trip round it	10 6	5 0	2 vols., 2s. each.	2 vols., 1s. each.
Michael Strogoff, the Courier of the Czar . .	10 6	5 0		
Dick Sands, the Boy Captain	10 6	5 0		
				s. d.
Five Weeks in a Balloon .	7 6	3 6	2 0	1 0
Adventures of Three Englishmen and Three Russians	7 6	3 6	2 0	1 0
Around the World in Eighty Days	7 6	3 6	2 0	1 0
A Floating City			2 0	1 0
The Blockade Runners .	7 6	3 6	2 0	1 0
Dr. Ox's Experiment . .			2 0	1 0
Master Zacharius . . .			2 0	1 0
A Drama in the Air . .	7 6	3 6		
A Winter amid the Ice .			2 0	1 0
The Survivors of the "Chancellor"	7 6	3 6	2 0	2 vols. 1s. each.
Martin Paz			2 0	1 0
THE MYSTERIOUS ISLAND, 3 vols. :—	22 6	10 6	6 0	3 0
Vol. I. Dropped from the Clouds	7 6	3 6	2 0	1 0
Vol. II. Abandoned . .	7 6	3 6	2 0	1 0
Vol. III. Secret of the Island	7 6	3 6	2 0	1 0
The Child of the Cavern .	7 6	3 6		
The Begum's Fortune . .	7 6			
The Tribulations of a Chinaman	7 6			
THE STEAM HOUSE, 2 vols.:—				
Vol. I. The Demon of Cawnpore	7 6			
Vol. II. Tigers and Traitors	7 6			

CELEBRATED TRAVELS AND TRAVELLERS. 3 vols. Demy 8vo, 600 pp., upwards of 100 full-page illustrations, 12s. 6d.; gilt edges, 14s. each :—
    (1) THE EXPLORATION OF THE WORLD.
    (2) THE GREAT NAVIGATORS OF THE EIGHTEENTH CENTURY.
    (3) THE GREAT EXPLORERS OF THE NINETEENTH CENTURY.

WALLER (*Rev. C. H.*) *The Names on the Gates of Pearl,* and other Studies. By the Rev. C. H. WALLER, M.A. Second Edition. Crown 8vo, cloth extra, 6*s.*

—— *A Grammar and Analytical Vocabulary of the Words in* the Greek Testament. Compiled from Brüder's Concordance. For the use of Divinity Students and Greek Testament Classes. By the Rev. C. H. WALLER, M.A. Part I., The Grammar. Small post 8vo, cloth, 2*s. 6d.* Part II. The Vocabulary, 2*s. 6d.*

—— *Adoption and the Covenant.* Some Thoughts on Confirmation. Super-royal 16mo, cloth limp, 2*s. 6d.*

Warner (*C. D.*) *My Summer in a Garden.* Rose Library, 1*s.*

—— *Back-log Studies.* Boards, 1*s. 6d.* ; cloth, 2*s.*

—— *In the Wilderness.* Rose Library, 1*s.*

—— *Mummies and Moslems.* 8vo, cloth, 12*s.*

Weaving. See " History and Principles."

Wills, A Few Hints on Proving, without Professional Assistance. By a PROBATE COURT OFFICIAL. 5th Edition, revised with Forms of Wills, Residuary Accounts, &c. Fcap. 8vo, cloth limp, 1*s.*

With Axe and Rifle on the Western Prairies. By W. H. G. KINGSTON. With numerous Illustrations, square crown 8vo, cloth extra, gilt edges, 7*s. 6d.* ; plainer binding, 5*s.*

Woolsey (*C. D., LL.D.*) *Introduction to the Study of International Law* ; designed as an Aid in Teaching and in Historical Studies. 5th Edition, demy 8vo, 18*s.*

Words of Wellington: Maxims and Opinions, Sentences and Reflections of the Great Duke, gathered from his Despatches, Letters, and Speeches (Bayard Series). 2*s. 6d.*

Wreck of the Grosvenor. By W. CLARK RUSSELL, Author of " John Holdsworth, Chief Mate," " A Sailor's Sweetheart," &c. 6*s.* Third and Cheaper Edition.

——————————— *v* Ɗ

London:

SAMPSON LOW, MARSTON, SEARLE, & RIVINGTON,

CROWN BUILDINGS, 188, FLEET STREET, E.C.